Permaculture Planting Designs

A handbook for creating a thriving, abundant garden

Pippa Chapman

Permanent Publications

Published by
Permanent Publications
Hyden House Ltd
13 Clovelly Road
Portsmouth
PO4 8DL
United Kingdom
Tel: 01730 776 582
Email: enquiries@permaculture.co.uk
Web: www.permanentpublications.co.uk

Distributed in North America by Chelsea Green Publishing Company,
PO Box 4529,
White River Junction,
VT 05001, USA
www.chelseagreen.com

Distributed in Australia by Peribo Pty Limited,
58 Beaumont Road,
Mt Kuring-Gai,
NSW 2080, Australia
https://peribo.com.au

Cover artwork and book design by Two Plus George Limited, info@twoplusgeorge.co.uk

Printed in the UK by Bell and Bain, Thornliebank, Glasgow

This product is made of material from well-managed FSC®-certified forests and from recycled materials and other controlled sources.

The Forest Stewardship Council ® (FSC) is a non-profit international organisation established to promote the responsible management of the world's forests. Products carrying the FSC label are independently certified to assure consumers that they come from forests that are managed to meet the social, economic and ecological needs of present and future generations.

British Library Cataloguing-in-Publication Data
A catalogue record for this book is available from the British Library

ISBN 978 1 85623 180 0

Praise for the book

Highly informative in a refreshingly down-to-earth, approachable manner. I get the feeling Pippa really wants to help the reader understand what they're doing and why, rather than giving them recipes about what they must do. The amount of information is phenomenal, about plants and design ideas. Always with the necessary background information. I warmly recommend this book both for beginners and knowledgeable gardeners.

Charles Dowding,
No dig organic gardener and author

Pippa has written the permaculture book I always wished existed; on one hand it overflows with practical ideas, case studies, and plant information – yet the book is so digestible and grounded that anyone reading this can and will be able apply what they've learnt to create their own dream spaces. I honestly feel this book is one of the most important contributions to permaculture in recent years, and it will have a permanent place in my design toolkit.

Huw Richards,
Permaculture gardener, author and YouTuber creator

Permaculture Planting Designs is packed with inspirational ideas and practical tips based on the author's many years of experience, for growing wildlife friendly polycultures, year round, whatever your space. From rentals and urban yards, to allotments and larger gardens, Pippa's adaptable and achievable designs, complete with detailed planting lists, will enthuse everyone to design and grow their own permaculture plot. This book will become a much used, soil stained addition to your gardening book shelf.

Stephanie Hafferty,
Award-winning garden and food writer,
and homesteader www.nodighome.com

A celebration of the achievable in forest gardening! Pippa writes from a place of experience, both in theoretical knowledge and in her extensive practice of creating forest gardens for her family and for clients. This book feels like Pippa is by your side, guiding you through the process of creating your own forest garden, with real life examples.

Liz Zorab,
Gardening broadcaster, author,
speaker and teacher

Many gardening books tell you how to grow plants, but very few show you how to grow a garden. That's why I'm so excited about Pippa Chapman's new book, *Permaculture Planting Designs*. Not only does she introduce you to dozens of useful, beautiful and unique plants, but she also shows you how to arrange them together in small patchwork plantings called guilds. Stitch these guilds together and you have your very own creative permaculture garden. This is organic gardening design made simple.

Tanya Anderson,
Lovely Greens

This book is an inspiration and a toolkit. *Permaculture Planting Designs* bridges the gap between theory and practice, offering clear principles, step-by-step guidance, and adaptable planting plans. Creating a planting design can be daunting, but these ready-made base plans are a brilliant starting point, helping to overcome that 'blank page' feeling and making permaculture planting design accessible. Inspiring anyone to create a diverse, beautiful and abundant garden. This is a book I'll be recommending widely to clients and students alike.

Sid Hill,
Multi award-winning ecological gardener,
designer and teacher

What makes Pippa's book invaluable is the wealth of hands-on gardening experience behind the creative designs. Any gardener will find inspiration here, whether they want to grow food (even if their garden is tiny and shady), attract pollinators, make natural remedies or craft using homegrown materials.

Vera Greutink,
Permaculture gardener, designer,
teacher and author

Designing a new planting scheme can be both exciting and daunting. There are so many considerations – site preparation, plant choices and combinations, as well as overall design. Pippa guides the reader through the process, breaking it down into clear, easy-to-follow steps. I particularly enjoyed exploring the wide range of ready-made examples Pippa includes as inspiration and as a starting point for your own design – from forest gardens, jam guilds, and perennial salad gardens to healing and skincare gardens, and even craft gardens – all complete with valuable plant lists. Whether you have a large plot, a small garden, or even just a balcony, there are ideas here for every space. This book is a valuable read for all gardeners, from novice to experienced – and one I know I will return to again and again.

Sally Morgan,
Garden writer and editor

Acknowledgements

The designs in this book have been so much fun to create and illustrate. I would like to say a huge thank you to Andrew, Poppy and Moss for never doubting that I would actually get it all done and for taking on all my household tasks to help me out when I needed it. It is a very special thing to have the support of those you love the most.

A big thank you to my sister Emma for being my target audience and therefore having to endure me firing endless ideas and thoughts her way. It was much appreciated.

I would also like to thank my fellow Aire Valley permies Katie, Lisa and Carla for their creative spirit, emotional support and wonderful road trip conversations. I am sure I have bored them to tears at times with all the trials and tribulations of writing a book.

My time as Permaculture Garden Manager at Esholt Hall Gardens was one of creative rediscovery and this book would have been much less diverse without my time designing there, so a big thank you to Paula, Chris and Nicola of Sponge Tree for allowing me the creative freedom to make a really special space for learning and wellbeing.

Thanks to Steph Hafferty and Liz Zorab who so generously shared their experience and wisdom of garden writing and self-employment and have helped me enormously on my journey as an author and educator.

And finally, thank you to the team at Permanent Publications, especially Maddy and Rozie, for giving me the opportunity to bring this book into the world and share my passion for plants and permaculture design; for embracing and encouraging me to do it in my own style; and for taking all my words and pictures and putting them together to create a beautiful book that I hope will inspire many others to design and create their own permaculture gardens. A huge thanks to Nicola, the brilliant book designer, for bringing everything together to look even better than I could have imagined. A special thanks to Tim, who is no longer with us, for believing in my ability before I did, and even though he is not here to see the finished book, he was in my thoughts throughout the whole journey.

About the Author

Pippa Chapman is an RHS-trained, award-winning garden designer, forest gardener, and permaculture educator. She runs a permaculture gardening and food forest design business, creates videos for her YouTube channel, and co-hosts the podcast, *Can I Dig it?* As the author of *A Plant Lover's Backyard Forest Garden* and a regular contributor to *Permaculture* magazine, she is passionate about helping people, complete beginners included, to transform their gardens into abundant, edible ecosystems.

Happiest when she's outdoors, Pippa loves designing, creating, and maintaining beautiful, ecologically diverse gardens. She delights in helping garden owners make the most of their space – whether large or small – while ensuring room for wildlife to thrive. With a background in ornamental horticulture and fine art, her edible planting designs combine productivity with beauty, creating spaces that provide food, habitat, and year-round visual appeal. Her particular passion is designing small-scale forest gardens that are as practical as they are enchanting.

www.youtube.com/@PippaChapmanPermaculture
www.thoseplantpeople.com
www.instagram.com/pippachapman_thoseplantpeople

© Neil Chapman

Contents

Introduction

The plant research part of the design process – I always relish this part

When I first had the idea to write this book I discounted it straight away. Permaculture design is all about following a design process reflecting on the three ethics and principles.* It involves surveying the person and the land, and analysing that information thoroughly and thoughtfully to come up with a design appropriate for both. Most importantly, the design is site specific. I have had so many conversations with gardeners wanting to include more edible and useful plants in their gardens but was met with the same problem each time. Despite all the books out there on the theory of forest gardens and permaculture gardening, many people are still too daunted to select from and combine the hundreds (or thousands) of plants listed in the books into a planting scheme for their garden.

I stand firm with my stance that you cannot apply a drag and drop approach to creating a permaculture garden, so this book has been designed to give a starting point, to show a series of example designs, but importantly to explain how to adapt these designs to suit your own wants and needs and the conditions in your garden. Just as a cookery book may give ideas for substitutions in a recipe, I give possible alternative plants within the designs. If a design is based around an apple tree and you don't like apples, you can substitute it for a pear or a cherry. These designs are for inspiration and can be planted in whole or in parts but, most importantly, are here to get you started on your polyculture adventure.

* Take a look at permaculture.org for more details about the permaculture ethics and principles

Why polycultures?

If we look at a natural landscape, plants grow as communities. Shade loving plants will fill the woodland floor, grasses and flowers will mingle together in meadows. Monocultures, plantings of single crops we see on most farms, don't exist in nature. The benefits of a diverse ecosystem are lost in an attempt to be efficient. Monocultures are more vulnerable to pests and diseases which can easily move from one plant to the next with no barriers to stop or slow them. If you mix plants together, as in nature, especially in a layered way such as in the form of a food forest, you can grow a more resilient community of plants. Scented plants mask the smell of the tasty plant a pest is looking for. Vegetation can physically block the spread of disease. In the unfortunate event that all of one type of plant succumb to attacks and provide no harvest (e.g. cabbage white butterflies have eaten all your cabbages) the other plants in the polyculture will fill the space left behind and provide a yield (e.g. apples from above the cabbages and alpine strawberries from the ground cover below them).

A wildlife design incorporates more than just plants for pollinators. Here I have included a pond and a dead hedge.

Companion planting

In its most simple form, companion planting is selecting two plants to create a beneficial relationship to help one or both of the plants to provide higher yields. There are several ways in which plants may support each other, such as providing nutrients, attracting beneficial insects, repelling pests or by improving growing conditions by offering shelter, shade, ground cover or structural support. Lists of companion plants have been circulating for many years with very little research to back up any claims but with plenty of anecdotal evidence. What works in someone else's garden may not work in your own. I have never found planting onions and carrots together to make any difference keeping slugs or carrot flies away. In fact I have seen slugs hungrily eating my onion tops. I prefer to use the lists, often falsely stated as factual, as a starting point to experiment and see what works for me.

Polycultures are a step up in complexity from companion planting by mixing two or more plants together to form a community of plants. These can be perennial or annual plants or a mix of both. Ideally the combination should provide mutual benefits to each plant, enabling it to grow more successfully than it would in a monoculture all by itself. In contrast to companion planting, which is usually one plant chosen to benefit another, polycultures are designed for each plant to benefit the whole planting scheme, as a natural ecosystem would function.

Polycultures are more difficult to manage and harvest, especially if you are a farmer using large machinery, but in our own home gardens this is less of a problem. The positives in terms of improved plant health, system resilience, benefits to wildlife and diversity of crops far outweigh any added effort during harvesting.

Sunflower 'Harlequin' and sea buckthorn have beautiful shades of orange

Guilds

Guilds differ from polycultures by focusing on one central element, usually a fruit tree, with the other useful plants chosen to support it. Food forests are often made up of several guilds joining together to create one large forest garden. Guilds are not always perennial. I have used a guild system in our polytunnel to support tomatoes. In this guild, tomatoes are the main crop we grow with all other plants chosen to improve the growing conditions for tomatoes whilst also providing another yield. We plant kale below the tomatoes in May which grows slowly until the tomatoes are removed in the autumn. The kale then has space and light to grow and crop through the winter. Having plants in the ground year round keeps soil life active and healthy and reduces the risk of soil borne diseases building up. Other crops we mix under the tomatoes include swiss chard, beetroot, lettuce, oriental salads and parsley.

The designs in this book are mostly polycultures with the occasional guild. Some are small food forest designs but I felt it important to include designs without the canopy tree layer as often trees are not suitable in a small space, create more shade than desired, are often not allowed on allotments or in rented gardens, and can get in the way of distant views or important sight lines. The next chapter will cover how to design your own polycultures and guilds to enable you to design your own useful and edible planting combinations, making the most of any beneficial relationships to create a thriving and beautiful ecosystem. The 13 designs are also provided if you get stuck and need some help and inspiration.

Getting to Know your Garden

Designing a new planting scheme, or whole garden, is such an exciting prospect: fresh, nutritious produce for use in the kitchen or home, that is grown in harmony with nature. What more could you ask for? You have read all the books, scribbled loads of notes but as you sit down, pen in hand to begin your design, the vast choice of plants and combinations can become overwhelming. It does narrow the choice somewhat if you are looking for edible and useful plants but you can find yourself with a huge list and no idea which will grow well in your garden or how to combine them into a design.

Take a deep breath and relax.

It is a common issue for even experienced gardeners. The part that often remains a struggle is the planting design. This book is here to help you through the process, breaking it down into easy to follow steps.

Collaging for my own garden has helped me to be more creative and capture all my ideas in one place

Survey – What do you have?

All good designs start with a survey. It simply means gathering information about your garden that you will need in order to choose the correct plants that will thrive in your space and to place them in the right location. If you have been in your garden for several seasons you may already know the sunny, shady and windy spots. If it's a new space, spend some time getting to know your plot at different times of day and in different weather conditions.

Your plan can be very rough and not to scale, the most important thing is that you have marked down all the information you need

Observations to mark on your plan:

- Which way is north?
- Where does the prevailing or most damaging wind come from?
- Which areas are shady and which are sunny?
- Which areas have damp soil and which areas have a tendency to dry out?

Mark these observations down on a rough plan, including any other points, such as important routes through the garden, sight lines and distant views. Do the paths/views work as they are or do they need rerouting or reframing? A well used practice in permaculture design is to observe for the first 12 months before making any decisions. This may be true for permanent features, such as buildings or ponds but planting schemes can always be tweaked later. If you are feeling cautious but impatient to get started, create an annual polyculture for the first year while you acquaint yourself with your new garden.

How well do you really know your garden? This planting looks lush but the soil is very dry.

What do you already have? Features such as a wildlife pond will determine what you position and plant nearby.

Exploring your soil

Have you explored your soil? You don't need to be a soil scientist to learn more about your soil type. A few simple tests can be done at home to determine your soil texture and structure in enough detail to decide which plants will grow well there. Permaculture teaches us to work with what nature provides, adding the minimum of inputs and it is best practice to choose the right plant for the right place rather than trying to change your soil type to suit the plants you want to grow. If you really want to grow a blueberry but have alkaline soil, a better option would be to grow it in a pot with ericaceous compost rather than try to change your soil pH.

Dig a test pit

The best way to get to know your soil is to get up close to it. Dig a hole in your garden to around the depth of your spade blade or 40cm. The ease with which you can push a spade into the ground will tell you a lot. If you use your foot on the spade to add extra force to get the spade into the ground and you are finding it difficult, this may be due to tree or shrub roots, rubble or very compacted soil. Only digging further will be able to answer this question.

As you dig down you may notice the soil changing colour.

Top soil

Top soil is the upper layer of soil that is rich in nutrients. It is made up of sand, silt and clay and also contains organic matter. This layer is where most of the biological soil activity takes place. It is usually dark brown in colour. It can be as little as a few centimetres deep but is usually 5-10cm in depth.

Subsoil

As you get to the subsoil, you will usually notice the soil change to a lighter colour. The subsoil layer is also made up of sand, silt and clay but with much less organic matter.

Bedrock

If you keep digging you will eventually reach a rocky layer called the bedrock. This is solid rock and may have a layer of many smaller rocks on top of it. For thin soils, the bedrock may be quite close to the surface. For some deep soils it may be several metres below the surface.

The depth of these different layers will determine the plants you can grow in your garden. Deep rich soils will support more plants and usually mean healthier plants. Thin rocky soils will limit the choice of plants but there are still plenty that will thrive in these conditions.

By digging a hole you can learn about your own soil. Is it rocky? Is it full of roots? Is it claggy and waterlogged? Is it sandy or like dust? Is it rich and dark and crumbly? All these observations will help you to build up a picture of the conditions you have and therefore the plants that are available to you in your design.

Jar test

You don't need to send your soil to a lab to find out what type it is. You can use a simple jar filled with your soil and some water to work out the ratios of sand, silt and clay that make up your soil. This is called soil texture and refers to the size of the soil particles.

- Sand particles are bigger than silt or clay particles. Sandy soils tend to be very free draining and struggle to hold on to water or nutrients but warm up easily
- Silt soils are fertile and free draining whilst also being moisture retentive. They can easily be compacted.
- Clay particles are very small and clay soils have a tendency to be heavy and waterlogged in winter and baked hard in summer. On a positive note, they are very fertile.
- Loam soil is a mix of sand, silt and clay with a better balance of good drainage, moisture retention and high fertility.

The jar test helps you to determine how well your soil will absorb and hold onto water and nutrients, allowing you to better select which plants are suited to your soil.

Collect your soil sample

You can take a few samples from around the garden and mix them together to get a general picture of your soil texture or I prefer to use several separate jars to get more detailed information from each bed. It is surprising how much soil composition can vary within a small area. Just remember to label each jar: e.g. bed under apple tree, raised vegetable bed, under kitchen window.

Scrape off any mulch and the top few centimetres of surface soil and collect a sample, ideally to a depth of around 10cm. Collect enough soil to fill your large jar half full. Top up the jar with water to around three quarters full and shake vigorously. If you have soil that is very dry or sticky, you may need to stir it to ensure all lumps of soil have dissolved.

Place the jar somewhere level and leave for at least 24 hours (clay particles may take over a week to fully settle) without disturbing it. In the first minute or so the sand and any grit should settle out as the large particles are the heaviest. Over the next hour or so, the silt will settle out as a separate layer on top of the sand layer. It can take another 24 hours or more for the clay particles to settle out, so be patient. You may get pieces of organic matter floating in the water. If the water is still opaque, leave it a bit longer. Once all the soil has settled, you can see the three different layers and determine your soil texture.

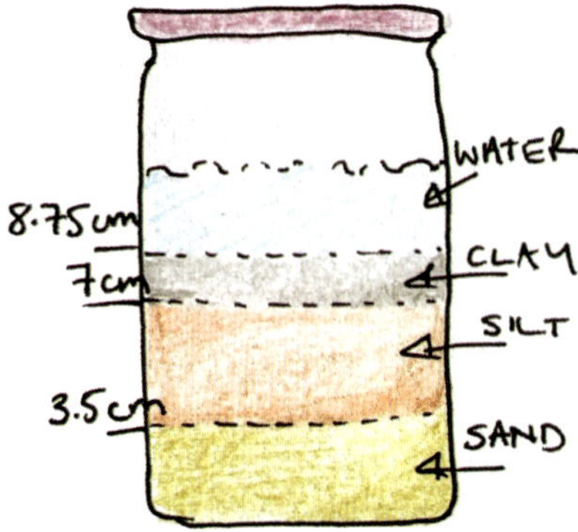

The change in layers can be hard to see but you should be able to make out the three layers

Calculate the percentage of each layer

If you use a jar with very straight sides, or even better a glass laboratory beaker, you can calculate the exact percentage by measuring the depth of each layer by using a simple calculation to find the percentage of each layer.

Divide the height of the layer by the total height of all the layers then multiply by 100. These figures can be plotted on a soil texture triangle (readily available online) to find your exact soil texture.

Height of layer / total height x 100 = percentage

An example:

clay layer in jar 1.75cm deep

silt layer 3.5cm

sand layer 3.5cm

total of all layers 8.75cm

sand layer 3.5cm / 8.75cm x 100 = 40%

silt layer 3.5cm / 8.75cm x 100 = 40%

clay layer 1.75cm / 8.75cm x 100 = 20%

(round all figures to nearest % to add up to 100%)

On the triangle, the lines cross in the loam section indicating a loam soil.

If you have 40% sand, 40% silt and 20% clay then congratulations, you have the highly prized loamy soil.

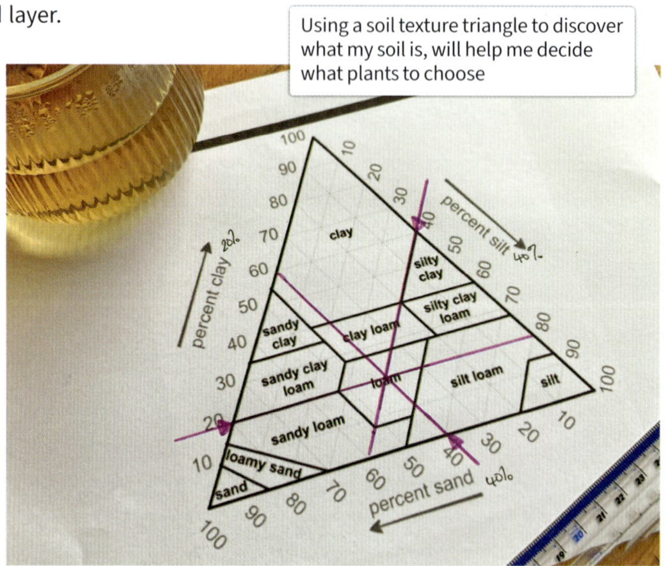

Using a soil texture triangle to discover what my soil is, will help me decide what plants to choose

Test the pH of your soil

You can purchase simple pH testing kits from most garden centres or online to get a reading of your soil pH although these are not always very accurate. My experience has also been that nutrient testing kits are fairly unreliable so a good supporting diagnosis method is to observe your plants and wider landscape.

Indicator plants suggest the soil type by their presence in the garden, although the presence of just one is not a definitive indicator. It's about building up a picture based on your garden and the wider landscape. Lush stinging nettles often indicate high nitrogen levels, rampant buttercups (*Ranunculus* sp.) often indicate damp soil. Rhododendron, azaleas and foxgloves growing well often indicates acidic soil. If they are struggling and have yellowing leaves, your soil is probably on the alkaline side.

Cow parsley indicates fertile soil in this woodland at Ecology Building Society, Silsden, West Yorkshire

Daisies growing in a lawn in a moorland garden where the soil is quite acidic

Meadowsweet usually grows in damp soil but here it is in quite a dry spot which is why it is important to build up a picture rather than use individual plants as an indicator

Indicator plants

Nutrient rich soil:

- Chickweed (*Stellaria media*)
- Cow parsley (*Anthriscus sylvestris*)
- Dandelion (*Taraxacum officinale*)
- Dock (*Rumex* sp.)
- Nettle (*Urtica dioica*)

Chalk or limestone:

- Betony (*Betonica officinalis*)
- Chicory (*Cichorium intybus*)
- Meadow cranesbill (*Geranium pratense*)
- Small burnet (*Sanguisorba minor*)
- Toadflax (*Linaria vulgaris*)

Acidic soil:

- Bilberry (*Vaccinium myrtillus*)
- Blueberry (*Vaccinium corymbosum*)
- Braken (*Pteridium aquilinum*)
- Daisy (*Bellis perennis*)
- Heather (*Calluna vulgaris*)
- *Rhododendron* sp.
- Sheep sorrel (*Rumex acetosella*)

Dry soil:

- Bugloss (*Anchusa arvensis*)
- Dyer's chamomile (*Cota tinctoria*)
- Spurge (*Euphorbia peplus* or *helioscopia*)
- Stonecrop (*Sedum* sp.)
- Thyme (*Thymus vulgaris*)

Damp soil:

- Creeping buttercup (*Ranunculus repens*)
- Lesser celandine (*Ficaria verna* subsp. verna)
- Liverworts and mosses
- Meadowsweet (*Filipendula ulmaria*)
- Mint (*Mentha* sp.)
- Rushes (*Juncus sp.*)

Improving your soil

Traditional advice to dig sand or gravel into a bed if you want to grow plants that need good drainage is outdated. My experience has been that massive amounts of gravel are needed to make a noticeable difference at huge cost to the environment from mining and transporting it. If you dig a planting pit in clay soil and fill it with gravel it will most likely become a sump and simply fill with water. If drainage is an issue and you desperately want to grow plants needing good drainage, create mounds or raised beds with added rubble, stones or gravel found on site or materials that are an output from another site nearby. This way you can lift the rootzone above the natural water level in the soil. Try to minimise the amount of imported mined materials.

You can have an impact on how well your soil drains and hold on to nutrients by adding organic matter to your soil. I practice no dig in my garden. I won't go into huge amounts of detail here but would like to emphasise that digging is very detrimental to soil life.

Our soil is teaming with life. Decomposers (microorganisms living in the soil) take dead leaves and plant matter and turn it into soil and nutrients which in turn feeds the plants. A whole food-web lives below the soil surface, decomposing organic matter, eating each other, breeding and dying and feeding our plants. We are discovering how important a healthy gut flora is for our own body's immune system and health; the same goes for the soil in our garden. There is an intimate relationship between the chemicals that plant roots exude into the soil and the microbes surrounding the roots who form a relationship with them. It is important to have something with roots growing in the soil year round so the microbes are always present and actively growing.

If the soil life is thriving then your plants are more likely to thrive. Forget the old tradition of synthetic plant feeds and build your soil instead. A nice deep mulch (layer) of organic matter each year will keep your soil healthy by providing food for the soil food web. This organic matter could be in the form of home made compost, well-rotted manure, leaves, straw, cut grass, bark chippings. Materials that will rot down and feed the soil. Organic matter helps to bind sandy soils together and improves water retention. Clay soils can be greatly improved by the addition of organic matter to open up the soil structure allowing better drainage and root penetration and preventing it from baking hard in summer.

I sometimes just improve the planting hole. A good mulch on top will then feed the soil without having to dig it over.

Dig once to improve very poor soil

As mentioned previously, I practice no dig but I do occasionally do a 'dig once' approach when starting a new garden if necessary. Worms and other soil life can take organic matter into the soil and relieve compaction but that can take years, if not decades. If you are starting with a very poor soil you could start by digging in well-rotted organic matter such as home made compost or manure then simply add more organic matter to the surface in future years in the form of a mulch. Roughly 5-10cm each year is ideal depending on the structure and organic content levels of your soil.

If you have all this information right at the beginning of the design process, it can prevent you wasting time putting together planting designs full of plants that won't like your soil type. That said, I am a big advocate for experimenting. Books and online catalogues often state a plant's preferred soil type but that doesn't always mean it wouldn't survive in other soils. So give things a try and move things around the garden until you find a spot where they are happy.

What are your wants?

Hopefully by now you have gathered enough information about your plot and soil to be able to select plants that will do well in your garden. The next step is to survey what you want (your desires) from the garden and to balance that with what you need.

Brainstorming

Brainstorming or collage on a piece of paper or in a word document are the most productive ways to gather this information. This process is about what you would like from your garden. These may be key words such as 'fruit for jam making', salads, flowers, social space, scent, winter interest. It may be in the form of images. I use collage and sketching in my brainstorming phase. This way I can gather ideas from magazines or online images and bring them all together on one page. This creative process helps me to process ideas and start to build up a picture of what I want from the design.

This may help me decide on things such as colour theme, planting style, features such as obelisks or water features. Looking through magazines and online image galleries is a very effective way to get over a creative block. At this point you are not refining ideas, you are just pulling out anything that catches your eye or ideas you have in your head. Once I have glued down all my images, I add text to my collages but you may find it is more helpful to use a spreadsheet or a mind map. Whatever you are most comfortable with, it is the generation and collection of ideas that is important in this phase.

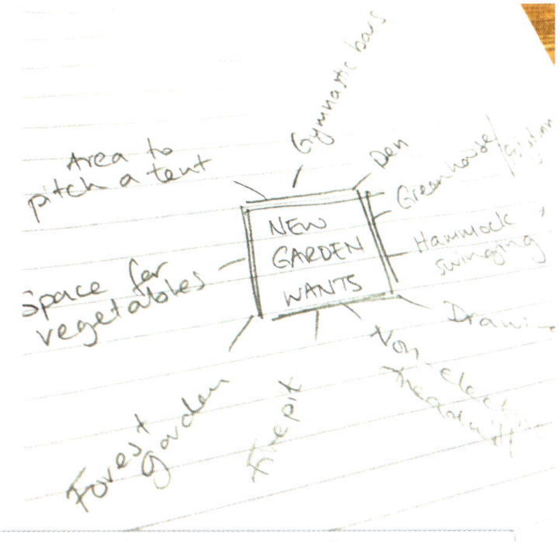

We use a mindmap to capture what we want as a family, then I can prioritise what we really need

What are your needs?

What function do you want the plants and garden to perform? The designs in this book are themed around different yields and functions. Is your priority wildlife, food, medicine, craft materials or a space to relax? I really enjoy working around a theme as it helps me to focus and narrow down my plant choices. Plants can of course tick many boxes at once. Plantain is both medicinal and edible. Lemon balm is medicinal, tastes lovely and is great for pollinators. You can maximise the amount of functions your planting design can fulfill by using a simple table or spreadsheet with the plant names along one edge and columns for each function along the other edge. This doesn't mean you should exclude a plant because it only ticks one box but it can be a useful exercise even if just to discover uses for a plant you hadn't known before. I recently discovered lamb's ear (*Stachys byzantina*) can be used as a natural plaster for garden first aid despite having used it in planting designs for nearly 20 years.

What do you like to eat? This may seem like an obvious question but one that is often overlooked. It is a good idea where possible to taste any of the more unusual herbs, fruit or vegetables before spending a lot of money on them. When I was first experimenting with forest gardens and perennial vegetables I spent a fortune on plants, such as sheep berry, Turkish rocket and salad burnet, none of which I enjoy eating. Through experimenting I did discover the flowers of the Turkish rocket are delicious and alive with clouds of pollinating insects in the summer, feasting on the pollen and nectar. The same goes for plants such as willow for weaving. Do your research and have a feel for how they flex and look once dried to make sure the plant you grow is the right one.

Even with common food crops such apples, the flavour spectrum varies more than most supermarket selections would suggest. Try to get along to apple or farm days to try before you buy, especially if you only have room for one tree. If jam making is your passion, plant more fruiting bushes. I discovered that I usually reach for the honey rather than jam with my toast so I don't need vast quantities of jam fruits. I grow some fruit to eat fresh and to add to fruit leather. Perhaps you are looking to stock up on herbal medical supplies and need to give more space to plants with healing properties.

In this border I have used a well-rotted mulch and am just digging it in wherever I dig a planting hole

High or low maintenance?

How much time can you dedicate to looking after your garden? If time is limited then perennial plants are less time consuming. They come back each year without having to sow seed, transplant and mollycoddle. If you love gardening and have limited space you may relish the challenge of trained fruit or intensive cropping annual vegetable polycultures. This may change over time. As my children grow and become more independent, I am finding I have more time for managing annuals amongst my perennial polycultures.

Once you have collected all this information about your site, soil and self, you can work out what this information tells you about your options. This stage is all about filtering out the plants and ideas that are not practical for your space, time or budget, and starting to identify the exact plants and features you do want. Let the designing phase begin.

Summary

- Make a plan of your garden
- Explore your soil
- Add observations to the plan – sunlight, soil conditions, wind direction, aspect
- Brainstorm for ideas – survey your wants and needs and make a list of desired plants

Planting Design

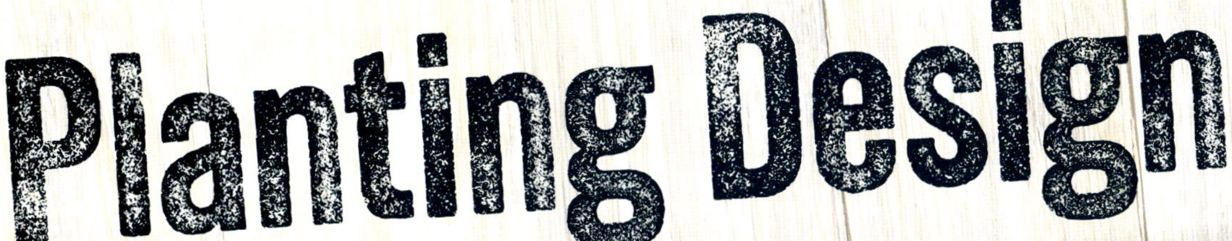

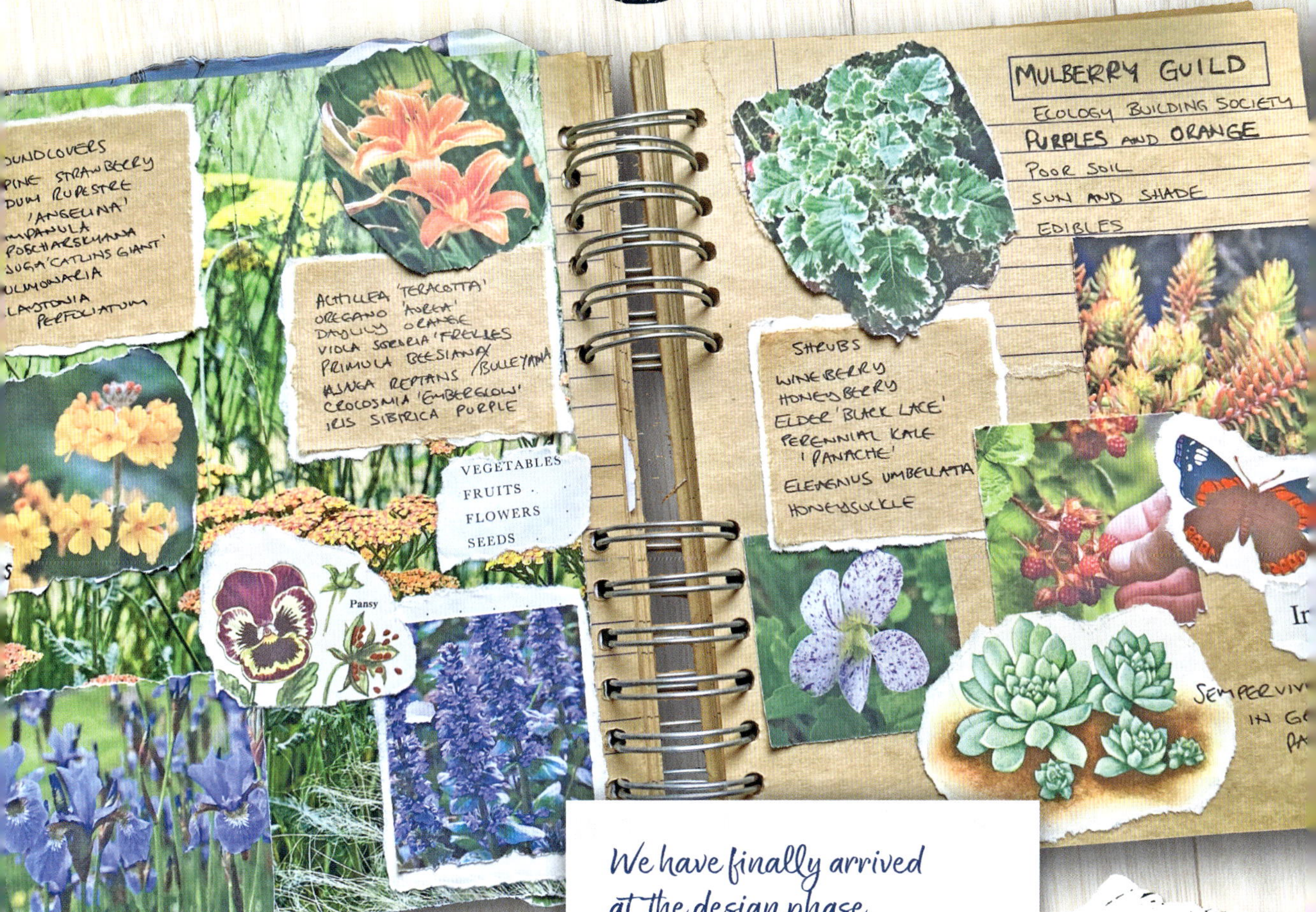

Brainstorming helped to get my wish list, now I will refine this into a final plant list by checking that each plant is going to like the soil and conditions

We have finally arrived at the design phase.

It is easy to jump right in here and rush to come up with a plan but the survey stage is vitally important if you want to have a successful design.

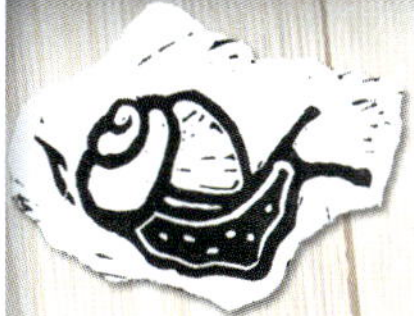

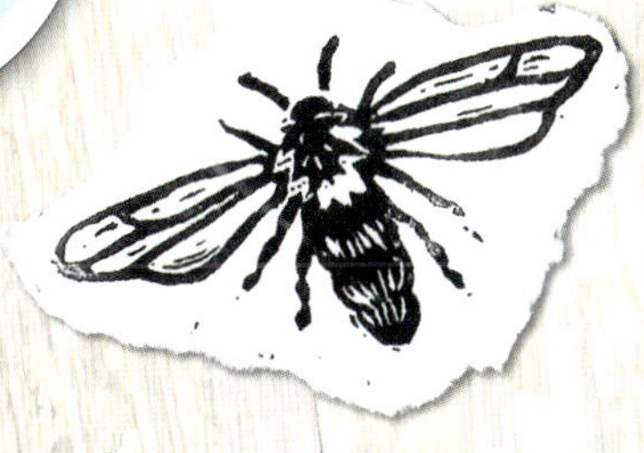

Creating a plant portfolio

The best way to choose the plants you want in your design is to create a plant portfolio. This is simply a place to gather information together to help you evaluate which plants will work and which will not. It could simply be a list or a whole page for each plant, depending on the time and energy you have for this stage. I'm a plant nerd so obviously I want a whole page for each plant with every bit of information I can find but that is not necessary for creating a design. The main information you need to gather is:

- Plant name – both common and botanical name
- Plant type, i.e. shrub, bulb etc.
- Plant dimensions – height and spread
- Growing conditions it can tolerate – boggy or free draining soil, sun or shade, windy or sheltered
- Plant use – food, medicine, pollinator plant etc.
- Flowering time and when to harvest.

These plants were chosen for this gravel garden because they will all happily grow in very free draining soil in full sun

I love to sit down and look through books to inspire my plant choices but there are also plenty of online resources if you don't have your own nerdy plant books

As you start to gather this information using your plant list from your brainstorm earlier, you will be able to whittle down your list as you discover which plants are suited to your garden and which are not. If you discover that most of the plants on your list are not suitable, you could try some further research either using online searches or the many plant encyclopedias available, to find plants that do like your conditions. Online forums are also a great resource as many people will have similar growing conditions as yourself and I always like to hear people's real life experiences of growing plants.

Your plant list will be different depending on the type of garden you want to design. If you are planting a food forest, you will want to make sure you have a good spread of plants for each vegetation layer (see family forest garden, p.27). If you are planting a garden for pollinators, you will want to make sure you have plants that flower in each month of the year. If you are looking to grow a salad garden, you will want salad leaves available year round. The best way to ensure you have achieved your goal is careful planning at this stage.

Plan for year round crops/interest/colour

Planning for balance throughout the year in terms of harvests and colour is something to consider and will help you narrow down your choices. Year round harvests mean you can supplement your diet from your garden, even if you don't achieve full self-sufficiency. This also avoids gluts, where you have a lot of one thing that requires preserving in some way and then needs room to store it. The promise of a harvest can also be the motivation you need to keep visiting your garden even in the colder and darker months. It is easy to keep on top of jobs if you are out in the garden, continually observing what is happening, noting any interventions needed and harvesting crops that are in season. If you find you have a 'hungry gap', a time where there are no crops to harvest, look up plants that are cropping at that time to fill the gap and find space for them in your garden.

The same applies for flowering plants. It is easy to keep visiting the garden centre in the summer months to buy something in flower that catches your eye, resulting in a short season of interest. It is very common for gardens to look amazing in June and July then burn out. Try to select at least a couple of plants for your design to be flowering each month of the year. Choice is more limited in the cooler months but the joy I get from seeing the few flowers that do appear in winter, despite the frost and short days, is immense. Winter aconites can freeze solid and recover fully the next morning, ready to attract brave bees venturing out on a mild spring day. Snowdrops can fill the space under deciduous shrubs and trees, flowering and dying down before the leaves appear on the trees. Miniature daffodils such as 'Hawera' and 'Angel's Breath' add fragrance to your garden as you potter about, looking to see what else is emerging as the milder weather arrives. (See pollinators garden p.112 for more details.)

It is not always possible to have as many plants flowering or cropping in the depths of winter as in mid summer but make sure you have at least some in each month.

Planning a garden for the National Trust at Shugborough. I wanted to have something scented flowering each month as they have visitors year round.

Beauty as a yield

There have been many studies now demonstrating the positive effects that green spaces and beautiful gardens can have on our mental health. By creating a visually appealing garden you are creating something to draw you into the garden. This is true even as an attractive view to gaze at through the window. Trying to achieve year round interest means this effect can be spread over as many months as possible with new and interesting plants blooming and fruiting as the seasons change.

Be less tidy

You may think that the above means keeping your garden neat and tidy, to make it attractive to look at. It is about a shift in how we think about our outdoor spaces. It gives me a huge sense of satisfaction to see piles of dead leaves, insect features full of dead stems and wild areas over the winter because I know what a huge difference it makes to supporting greater biodiversity in the garden. If you really struggle to embrace the wilder look of a permaculture garden, use evergreen shrubs to mask your dead hedge or wild corner. You can enjoy the view of the shrubs whilst wildlife enjoys the space underneath and behind them.

Colour and style

Style is absolutely a personal thing. I have created gardens I love that others couldn't live with. I have visited famous gardens with great reviews that have left me cold as they are so over manicured. Your garden should be whatever you want it to be. People often assume a permaculture garden must be messy and wild but there is no reason for that. It's just the usual aesthetic we expect. Symmetry is not natural looking but that doesn't mean it can't be applied in permaculture garden design. It doesn't affect how the plants grow or how abundant the harvests will be. You may want to carefully consider scale and proportion or you may want to create a jumble of plants thrown together purely based on their requirements. You could use shapes such as spirals or mandala circles or have orderly straight lines. Go with whatever brings you joy.

The same goes for colours. Some love the calm of muted shades of blue, purple and white; others love the vibrant fiery reds, oranges and yellows while others love an explosion of clashing colours. The beauty of having a design which changes with the seasons is that you could have all of the above in one garden. I have designed a few gardens where the spring colour scheme is purples and yellows blending into yellows and pinks for summer then into pinks and oranges in the autumn.

How to combine plants

This is the part of the design process that people are the most hesitant to start. How do you know which plants will grow well together? By trying it out. Successful designers have years of experience and they also sometimes get it wrong. There are so many variables that a combination that works well in one garden, may not do so well in next door's garden thanks to changes in soil moisture, fertility and light levels. The only way to really know is to experiment in your own space.

The main things you need to know when combining plants are the dimensions and the habit of the plant. Is it tall and upright or short and sprawling, or tall and sprawling, or short and compact? By knowing these traits of the plant, we can decide if they might be a good fit together. It can be good to break up a sea of plants of the same height with some taller plants dotted about. You don't always have to plant tall plants at the back of a border. Just take into account any shade that tall plants may throw across the bed throughout the day.

If you are adding trees and large shrubs, you can plant under them, so keep this in mind when drawing the eventual size of the tree canopy onto your plan. This area should not be left bare. Take a look at some of the designs in this book if you want an example of how this looks.

I sometimes plan the structure of a border but often I like it to look more natural so I mix the heights up a bit more

Mixing *Salvia* 'Caradonna', lamb's ear (*Stachys byzantina*), kale 'Taunton Deane', *Ammi majus* and buddleja 'Buzz Candy Pink' gives flowers for a long period

An edible polyculture of *Smyrnium perfoliatum*, camassia and a dwarf apple tree

If you are still feeling unsure, give each plant a little bit more space than they need to start off with, that way you can reduce the likelihood that one will kill off another. Observe how they grow and be prepared to move plants about at the end of the first growing season if you don't feel they are happy together. The main problem encountered is that one plant is more vigorous than the other and its foliage starts to smother the weaker plant. You may just need to move them a bit further apart.

The other reason for moving a plant is that it is not happy where you put it. Even if you have made sure it is supposed to grow well there, you checked it has enough sun or shade, and the soil conditions are right, if it looks like it's struggling, I would try it elsewhere. Herbaceous plants are easy to move, shrubs can be cut back and transplanted but you may need to start again with a tree. If a tree doesn't get a good start, it is less likely to be healthy in the long term, even if you move it. This is why I always suggest starting with adding the tree and shrub layer to your design first. These are the most important elements to get right first time.

Below I will cover guild design which is focussed around a main tree or shrub (the keystone species). If you are wanting to design a purely herbaceous design without a main keystone species (a tree or a shrub) then consider what Is your most important plant, the one you couldn't do without, and make that the first plant you add to the design. Add plants next to this main plant, one at a time, ideally repeating the blocks of each type of plant for added resilience and rhythm, and slowly build up a design working from this main plant, outwards. Consider things like which plants would do best along the front edge without sprawling onto the path or lawn too much. Have the plants you want to harvest the most often, closer to the front in easier to reach places. Do you need to add extra paths, keyhole beds or stepping stones to be able to harvest easily?

Creating your planting designs

As a brief reminder, a polyculture is simply a mix of two or more crops grown together in one space at the same time, ideally for mutual benefit. Companion planting is an example of polyculture growing. A guild is a collection of plants (often around a central tree or shrub) chosen for their specific benefits to the whole group.

Forest gardens are a type of multilayered perennial polyculture where useful plants are grown in a naturalistic way inspired by the structure and ecology of a natural woodland.

Here I explain how to create a guild. This guild may include trees and shrubs but it doesn't have to.

Repetition in design

I like to design these smaller groupings of plants, then put them together to create larger planting designs. An acre food forest design could be created from multiple guilds added together. This breaks the design down into manageable blocks. I will sometimes repeat a guild a few times within a larger design as it creates a sense of visual rhythm. This also means the design is more resilient as you have multiples of each plant; if one dies, you have a backup. It also means you have more to harvest. If you only have one plant of thyme, you are likely to strip it of all its foliage to meet your needs. If you have three plants, you can pick a bit from each one in rotation. This holds true within your guild too. Rather than one of each plant, add a block of three or four of each plant to make your design more resilient.

Visually, repetition and rhythm are two design techniques used in ornamental design to create a cohesive design. You may not want your planting to look too 'designer' but there is something very visually satisfying about a garden that feels like a curated design rather than a chaotic and haphazard mix of plants. You don't necessarily need to repeat the same plant but you could consider repeating colours. For example, adding a dark leaved elder, purple hazel, red amaranth, mountain spinach with its shimmering purple splashes on its leaves and a purple flowered dahlia means you have plants with similar colours to hold the design together. If these are dotted around the design amongst the other plants, it will make the whole design more cohesive, even though they are different plants.

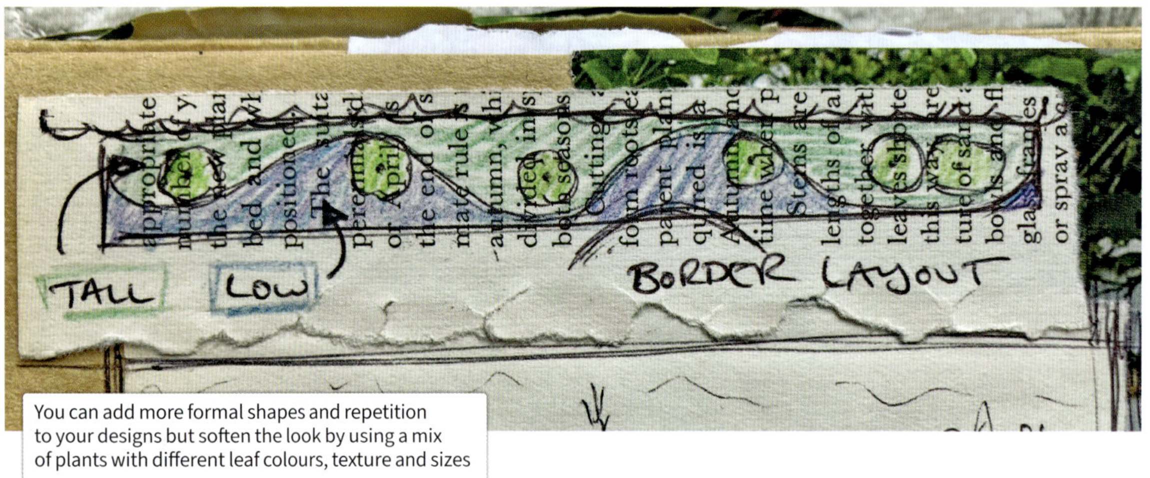

You can add more formal shapes and repetition to your designs but soften the look by using a mix of plants with different leaf colours, texture and sizes

Play with placements method

You may wish to try the paper circle design method. It takes a bit of time to cut everything out but it can be a brilliant way to try out endless combinations without having to keep rubbing out your sketch. It is much more fun than sitting and procrastinating.

Cut out various circles (to the same scale as your base map/plan) using the spread of the plant to determine the circumference of the circle. For ease of designing, you may wish to cut out circles to depict a group of smaller plants, for example a 1m circle may fit in 10 or more alpine strawberry plants or three or four daylilies. Make sure you label the circle with the plant name and it may be helpful to include the height. When designing with community groups, I have found it helpful to use different coloured paper for different heights to make it easy to identify the different layers. Green for ground covers, yellow for up to 50cm, orange for 0.5–1m, red for 1-1.5m, purple for 1.5-2m, blue for 2m+.

The forest garden plan for Bedford fields forest garden in Leeds. Later additions are stuck onto the original plan.

Move these circles around your plan until you find a combination you are happy with. Remember that where you are including trees or shrubs, the circles can overlap. You may find it helpful to use small pieces of sticky tack to hold the circles in place until you are happy with the final arrangement. Then stick the circles down and you have your final design.

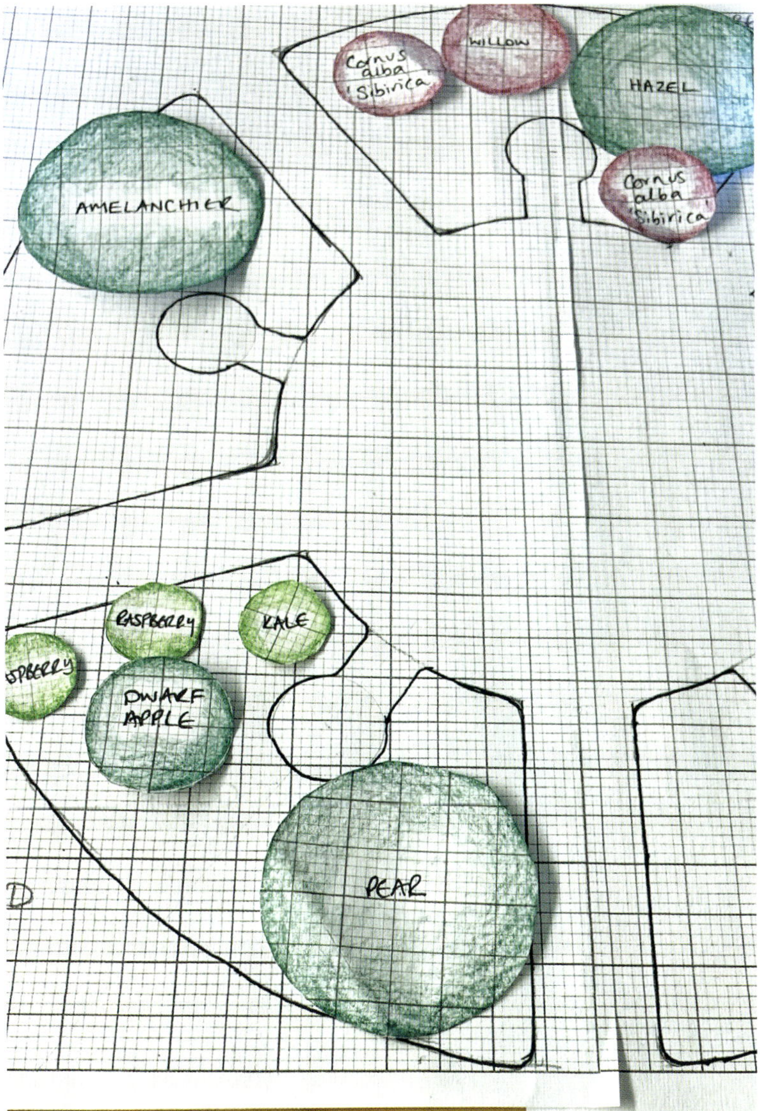

Guild design

Make up of a guild

A plant guild is a selection of plants that work together to support one another, mimicking natural ecosystems. Each plant should contribute a function, to support the main keystone plant or plants, such as fixing nitrogen, attracting pollinators or providing shade. Guild design gives you a nice easy formula to use to begin to put together your combination.

The main elements of a guild are:

A keystone species

The primary crop, usually a tree or shrub. You can add in secondary crop plants to get multiple yields from one guild.

Suppressor plant

Ground cover plants for weed suppression and to help retain soil moisture.

Attractor plants

To bring in beneficial insects and attract pollinators for natural pest control.

Repellers/confuser plants

To repel and confuse pests, due to their strong smell, to keep them away from the main plant.

Mulchers

Dynamic accumulators that bring nutrients up from deep in the soil and add them to the soil surface as they die back.

Fertility plants

Nitrogen fixing plants have special bacteria living in their roots which can take nitrogen from the air and convert it into a form that plants can use to grow.

Using paper cutouts to decide where to place the tree and shrub layer for the Esholt Hall Gardens mandala forest garden

Clover 'Purpurascens quadrifolium' (*Trifolium repens*) is a nitrogen fixing ground cover plant

Autumn olive (*Elaeagnus umbellata*) is a large shrub that fixes nitrogen and produces a crop of edible berries

Begin by choosing your keystone species, this is typically a fruiting or nut bearing tree but could also be a shrub such as blackcurrant or jostaberry.

Next choose at least one of each of the following: a suppressor plant, an attractor plant, a repeller plant, a dynamic accumulator and a fertility plant.

Add these to your plan around the main keystone plant. You may decide to choose a few plants for each category to bring diversity and resilience to your design. You may find that some plants fit in more than one category. Self-heal (*Prunella vulgaris*) is both an effective ground cover and fantastic plant for pollinators. I personally feel that the effects of the repeller plants are a bit overstated, especially when working with trees. Chives around the base of a tree may deter deer, but not if it's very hungry. Nasturtiums reportedly repel codling moths but if you have a large tree and a small nasturtium I am not sure how effective this will be.

The same rules apply for a guild as for any other design. Make sure the plants you choose will be happy with the amount of sunlight or shade you are giving them. Plant shade loving plants on the north side of trees and shrubs, and sun loving plants on the southern side. That is assuming that your guild is not in the shade of larger trees or buildings. If so, all your plants will need to be shade tolerant.

Nitrogen fixers improve the fertility of the soil

The science around how or if these plants share their nitrogen with other plants is still under research but generally the understanding is that you need to chop and drop or coppice a nitrogen fixing plant for it to make the nitrogen available to the other plants.

- Alder (*Alnus cordata*)
- Black locust (*Robinia pseudoacacia*)
- Clover (*Trifolium repens*)
- False indigo (*Amorpha fruticosa*)
- Judas tree (*Cercis siliquastrum*)
- Oleaster (*Elaeagnus angustifolia*, *E.* x *ebbingei*, *E. umbellata*, *E. commutata*)
- Orange bladder senna (*Colutea* x *media*)
- Sainfoin (*Onobrychis viciifolia*)
- Scotch broom (*Cytisus scoparius*)
- Sea buckthorn (*Hippophae rhamnoides*)
- Siberian pea tree (*Caragana arborescens*)
- Spanish broom (*Spartium junceum*)

Yarrow attracting many insects to the wildlife border of the mandala forest garden at Esholt Hall

Attractor plants bring in beneficial insects and attract pollinators

Blackcurrant (*Ribes nigrum* cultivars)

Crocus, spring-flowering (*Crocus vernus* are good in turf or borders)

Globe thistle (*Echinops ritro*)
'Veitch's blue' is shorter around 1m, plant *E. bannaticus* if you want something taller at around 1.8m

Grape hyacinth (*Muscari armeniacum*)

Hebe cultivars

Hellebore (*Helleborus* sp.)

Hylotelephium – 'Purple Emperor' is a late-flowering cultivar (previously known as sedum)

Lungwort (*Pulmonaria* sp.)

Primrose (*Primula* sp.)
P. rosea flowers in late winter/early spring, *P. veris* in spring, *P. pulverulenta* flowering into mid-summer

Red bistort (*Bistorta amplexicaulis*) 'Rosea' or 'Firetail'

Yarrow (*Achillea millefolium*)

See pollinators garden (p.111) for more ideas.

Suppressor plants cover the ground and prevent weeds growing

Alpine strawberry (*Fragaria vesca*)

Dwarf comfrey (*Symphytum grandiflorum*) – cultivar 'Hidcote Blue' flowers for months

Siberian bellflower (*Campanula poscharskyana*)

Violet (*Viola* sp.) – *Viola sororia* 'Freckles' forms a dense mat and has edible flowers

Repellers/confuser plants repel and confuse pests to keep them away from main plant

Lemon balm (*Melissa officinalis*)

Mint (*Mentha* sp.)
Garden mint – *M. spicata*, apple mint – *M. suaveolens*, peppermint (*Mentha* x *piperita*)

Rosemary (*Salvia rosmarinus*)

Mulchers/dynamic accumulators bring up nutrients and redeposit them

The research behind these plants is also still ongoing. Some suggests that they may actually rob nutrients from the surrounding plants. If used as plants to chop and drop in situ then you are helping to build soil organic matter which is a good thing. If you do add them to your design, remember to cut them and use their leaves as a mulch at least once a year.

Chicory (*Cichorium intybus*)

Dandelion (*Taraxacum officinale*)

Lamb's quarters (*Chenopodium album*)

Meadowsweet (*Filipendula ulmaria*)

Nettles (*Urtica dioica*)

Rhubarb (*Rheum rhabarbarum*)

A guild built around a large fruited hawthorn (*Crataegus arnoldiana*) with rhubarb, blackcurrant, strawberries, Good King Henry, sweet cicely, clover and *Brunnera macrophylla*

Expanding your guild

If you want to create a larger planting design you can design multiple guilds then join them together to create a larger food forest design. This helps to make a large empty space feel less daunting and ensure you have covered the functions needed, such as plants to attract natural pest control spread evenly throughout your larger design.

Planning for succession

As the trees and shrubs mature, the growing conditions beneath the tree will change as the area of shade expands. This may mean changing some of the planting immediately below the trees after about five years. As your garden develops, some plants will do too well, becoming invasive whilst others will struggle or die. Permaculture gardening is about a constant process of observation and tweaking so you could create a second design in five years time or you could just observe your garden, making notes each year, and modify the planting as needed.

Creeping comfrey is loved by bees, is a great ground cover plant and can also be cut and the fresh leaves used as a mulch

Allium moly grow under some trees to give colour and a crop while I decide what else to add to the design

Summary

- Create a plant portfolio
- Decide on a style and colour scheme if desired
- Try to achieve year round interest/harvests/ flowers
- Play with placements until you find combinations you are happy with
- Put smaller groups together to create larger scale planting designs

How to design with this book

How to adapt the ready made designs for your own garden

The designs in this book have been created to provide inspiration and as a starting point for your own designing. If you would like to use one of the designs in your own garden, you will more than likely need to make some modifications to suit your site. The plants in the designs should suit a wide range of soil types and conditions, unless you have an extreme such as deep shade, dry or boggy soil. The most likely issue might be that the design may not fit with your needs or the dimensions of your plot. If the dimensions are the issue, plants within the design can be moved around to create a new combination. If needs are the issue, plants that meet your needs can be added to the design in place of, or as well as, those that are not so useful to you.

I would still suggest you follow the design process of getting to know your garden and your needs and to create a base map to work from. This is the best way to ensure the design is suitable for your garden. If you want to use the plant list but in a different combination, start as you would with the design process but skip the plant portfolio stage as that has already been created for you. It is still important to check the conditions each plant likes to ensure they will all thrive in your own garden's specific microclimate. Any that won't be happy can be substituted.

If you make your base map to the same scale as the plans in the book, you could photocopy the design and cut some of the plants out to try the 'playing with placement' technique discussed earlier. You may like to scan a design to create a photocopy or upload to a drawing app to scribble and move things about. I have often used a piece of tracing paper to overlay the original design so it is easy to see the design below but you end up with a sketch that is much neater and less cluttered with scribbles.

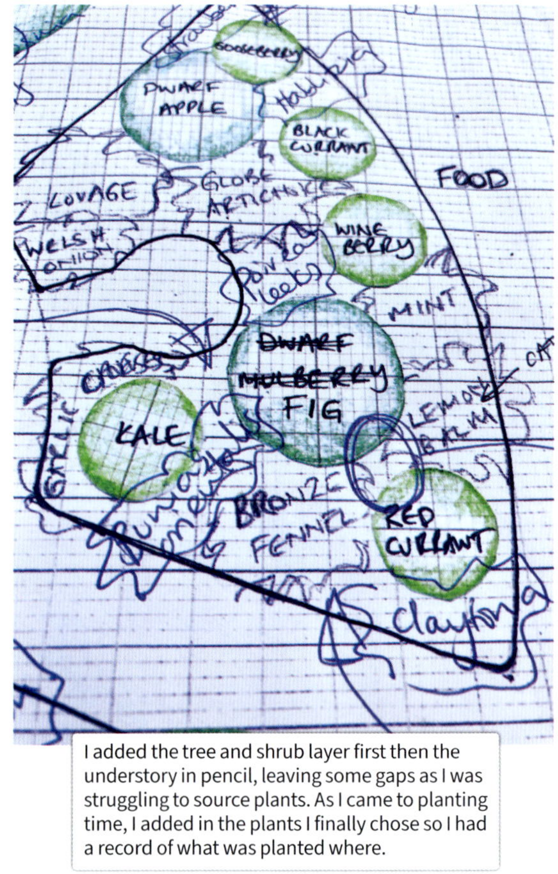

I added the tree and shrub layer first then the understory in pencil, leaving some gaps as I was struggling to source plants. As I came to planting time, I added in the plants I finally chose so I had a record of what was planted where.

Place larger plants first

Just as with designing from scratch, when modifying designs start with placing the trees and shrubs as this will tell you where the shade will be in the garden. Then place the lower layer plants around and under the trees. You can position the plants from the shady areas in the new shady areas. And those from the bed edge can be repositioned along the new edge. You can add in additional plants that don't feature in the original design and take out those you don't want. You may like to give this a try as a practice step to help you build confidence before you create your own unique and bespoke design for your own plot.

You can add smaller designs together to make a larger design

Plant substitutions

I have been asked a few times what exact plants you should put around an apple tree to help it grow better. You don't need to be too worried about these precise combinations. If you don't like apples, swap it for a pear or a plum and the rest of the design will still be just as happy, although take note of the eventual spread of any substituted plants in case you need to amend the adjacent planting.

If you want to remove a plant, you could simply plant extra of whatever is next to it or substitute a plant of similar size and habit, e.g. a blackcurrant could be swapped for a redcurrant or a gooseberry. Mint could be substituted with lemon balm or bee balm. As with any design, you can never be one hundred percent sure a plant will be the right choice until you give it a try.

Joining designs together

The designs in this book could be joined together or planted in isolation in different areas of your garden. You can choose to combine different smaller designs to create one larger design. Where designs meet, you may need to merge the planting together. This can be achieved by making blocks of each alternate edge plant a little larger to create a wavy edge, then fitting the two together a bit like a jigsaw. Check to ensure that you are not creating shade for areas of sun loving plants in a neighbouring design and substitute for more suitable plants where necessary.

Garden layout and features

The focus of this book is the planting design but I wanted to add a few notes about garden design before delving into the plants. I have transformed many gardens simply by keeping the layout as it is and changing the planting. However if you feel the layout of your garden is not working, the best time to rethink this is before you plant up your new scheme.

Dramatic changes can be achieved by simply changing the shape or size of your borders, or the route a path takes through the space. If you have a lawn, it is usually fairly simple to turn that into planting beds. If you have paving, tarmac, concrete or gravel with hardcore foundations then the change is more difficult to make. If you decide to remove or remodel hard landscaping features such as these, consider how you might be able to reuse that waste within the garden. The rubble could possibly be used to build walls, bed edges or as the foundation for a new path, patio or garden building.

Access into beds for harvesting is something that needs careful thought. Most ornamental borders are designed to be viewed from the edge rather than allowing you to walk in amongst the plants. Whilst stepping stones can provide a hard surface without taking up too much of the planting area, these can soon disappear under a sea of foliage in summer. My favourite solution is to add a keyhole bed, named for their distinctive shape. It consists of a narrow path with a larger circle at the end to allow you to turn around and maybe put down a basket while you harvest. This allows easy access without taking up the space of a continuous path.

A dramatic change can be achieved by simply changing the shape of the borders without any earth moving or hard landscaping. Keyhole beds allow access for harvesting.

Shapes of borders and paths

The shapes within your garden can change the feel of the space. Angular shapes can offer a nice contrast to the softness of the plants but tend to feel less relaxing than curved shapes. A straight path is very efficient and can be perfect for a path that joins two places such as where you park your car and your front door. A more curved and meandering path may be preferable in a foraging space to encourage you to slow down, observe the garden and any plants that are ready to harvest and to maximise access to the crops.

I always prefer natural materials within the garden as they blend in with the planting better. In my own garden I use whatever I have lying around or materials others are getting rid of. To edge my beds I have used a mixture of old scaffolding planks, large branches, rotting logs, woven willow hurdles, broken paving slabs on their edge and stones dug out of the ground. You don't need anything to edge your beds, you could simply have a small trench at the edge of the lawn to prevent the grass from encroaching on the planting; it comes down to what you have available and what style you are wanting to achieve.

I love weaving bed edges with willow cut from the garden

Materials

Path surfaces are another consideration. Mown turf paths can be high maintenance and the turf can be ruined in winter if the ground is wet but they do look lush and green and the cut grass can be used as a mulch around the plants. Bark chippings are another popular choice. I chip my own branches to keep my bark paths topped up but the bark does rot down so will need topping up every couple of years. Once broken down, the bark from the paths can be used as a mulch on beds before a new layer is added to the path.

Hard surfaces such as paving or compacted gravel can be very practical, needing little maintenance but are very high input and expensive. I removed some patio paving slabs to create more planting space and I reused the slabs for a new path. I chose to pave the section that is used the most in winter, from the house to the polytunnel, as the bark path was getting quite muddy and waterlogged on this stretch. The rest of the garden is made up of bark paths and existing paved areas. If you have the right soil type, you can get away with compacted soil paths and manage them by hoeing but they will get very muddy in wet weather.

A totally different approach is looking to nature, to a natural woodland where we may be foraging for food and notice there are no paths. You may decide to abandon any type of structure or boundary in your garden and simply include sections of ground covers that don't mind being trampled periodically. You may enjoy hacking your way through the shrubs (chopping and dropping as you go) and wading through the herbaceous layers to access crops at harvest times and the rest of the year leave it to the wildlife. All these choices are yours to make and the included pre-made designs or your own designs can be worked around these shapes and features.

As a final note, you may want to add signs and plant labels to your garden to help educate others about the plants and their uses, or about management techniques to increase biodiversity and habitat. Even if your garden is not on public view, you can inspire friends, family and neighbours to start to garden in a different way.

Campanula poscharskyana is a brilliant ground cover with edible leaves and flowers

Summary

- Are you happy with your current layout or would you like to make changes?
- Do you want to include more paths or keyhole beds for easier access for harvesting?
- What materials would you like to use for your paths or boundaries?
- When using these designs, check each plant in the list is suitable for your garden.
- Decide on any plant substitutions, check they will like your soil and microclimate.
- Rearrange plants within the planting plan to suit the size and shape of your plot. Pin down the location of any trees and shrubs first, then the lower layers.
- Ensure any relocation of plants does not cause shade for sun loving plants.

Family
Forest Garden
BUNDANT
FOOD
The best thing about growing a forest garden in your own backyard is that it can be just as beautiful as a regular garden but can feed your family too.
FUN

Forest gardening is a method of growing a diversity of edible, mostly perennial, plants in layers which mimic a woodland, taking inspiration from its structure and ecosystems. By working with nature we can create low maintenance and productive gardens which are a haven for wildlife and ourselves. Plants are chosen for their functions and yields and placed according to their size to create a garden where the plants support each other rather than compete. By encouraging beneficial creatures such as pollinators, frogs, ladybirds and ground beetles into the garden, outbreaks of pests can be managed by nature instead of using harmful sprays. The diversity of wildlife is one of the first changes you notice as you plant a forest garden. We can grow our food in a way that supports wildlife rather than tries to exclude it.

A yard polyculture for the children to forage in

The structure of a forest garden

The makeup of a young woodland can be broken down into seven layers. Each layer occupies a different part of the vertical space within a garden, so the plants are not competing for growing space. There is no strict rule that says you need to include all seven layers to call it a forest garden. It is an ideal but not a necessity, especially on a smaller scale where all seven layers can be difficult to achieve. My approach is that it is more important what we learn from the pattern of how a forest grows in nature, its ecology, layering and nutrient cycling, rather than trying to tick seven boxes.

An understory layer of variegated kale 'Daubentons Panache', my youngest loves to pick and eat the leaves raw

Seven layers of a forest garden

1. **Canopy layer**

These are the tallest trees, such as nut trees, native trees such as oak and alder or large fruit trees. In small gardens this layer is usually absent.

2. **Lower tree layer**

Dwarf fruit and nut trees, such as apple and hazel, under 3m in height

3. **Shrub layer**

These are commonly currant bushes, evergreen shrubs such as mahonia or raspberries.

4. **Herbaceous layer**

These are the plants that grow each year then die right back to ground level in the winter, unless they are evergreen. They have no permanent branch structure.

5. **Ground cover layer**

These plants hug the ground. They are spreading plants that grow along the soil surface and cover the bare ground.

6. **Rhizosphere**

Many think of the soil surface as the lowest layer however many plants have edible roots, tubers, bulbs and corms.

7. **Climbing plants**

Plants in this group climb through all the other layers, to make the most of all the available vertical space. They can also be grown up an obelisk or rope.

Forest gardens are predominantly perennial plants, such as fruit and nut trees, fruiting bushes, herbs and perennial vegetables. This makes them very resilient as a growing system as they will grow and produce harvests each year with minimum effort. This perennial aspect has been a hugely beneficial trait during many busy periods of my life when time for tending a garden has been scarce. The perennial plants still sprung up from the earth regardless of my neglect and gave a yield.

Family friendly food forest

As they grow, the children can help with harvesting rather than just foraging for their own snacks

Dehydrated apple rings are still a family favourite even as teenagers

When I was pregnant with my first child, Poppy, I had visions of tending the vegetable garden with her in a sling and carrying on as normal. The reality did not match the dream. With a child who never slept and chronic exhaustion, I had little spare energy for growing annual vegetables. By the time my second child, Moss, came along, who also never slept, we had luckily already converted the yard to perennial fruit, herbs and vegetables creating a mini forest garden.

This space has been wonderful for us as a family. We taught our children to forage, showing how to tell the alpine strawberries were ripe by squeezing them gently as they often turn red before they are ripe. Hard means not quite ready, soft means ready to stuff in your mouth. We grew peas over archways so they could pick them easily but also ride their bikes in a circuit through the flowerbed. They have been excited to dig up the jewel like tubers of oca and munched on kale picked straight off the bush. As the children have grown, we have adapted the garden a bit each year. We have recently moved and the new requests are a hammock and a fire pit which will be used just as much by us as by the kids.

I have designed this family friendly mini forest garden for the whole family to enjoy with easy foraging for small children and places to play whilst also including habitat for wildlife and colour and interest to ensure it is beautiful, productive and fun. All the plants in this design can be eaten so are safe for small children to forage. This foraging should be done with supervision until they are old enough to know what they can and shouldn't eat but if they did become curious, none of the plants are toxic if nibbled accidentally. Even the apple and blackcurrant leaves are okay to eat, although only in small amounts, but it is best to direct your child towards the fruits, berries, edible flowers and salad leaves. Start with small amounts to check for any allergies. Teaching your child how to forage is a fantastic way to get them interested in growing their own food and spending time outdoors.

Plant list

Listed in layer order

Dwarf apple (*Malus domestica*)

M27 rootstock will grow to a height of less than 2m with a spread of around 1.5-2m. This is a perfect height for children to reach. Due to its dwarfing nature that suppresses its vigour, it will need staking. A good self-fertile variety is 'Saturn' but there are many other suitable varieties.

Raspberry 'Autumn Treasure' (*Rubus idaeus*)

This is a great self-supporting raspberry growing to around 1.5m. I simply tie the canes together at the top to give extra support once the fruit starts to ripen and the canes bend over. If you have small children and want a shorter variety to allow them to reach the fruit, 'Ruby Beauty' is only 1m in height.

Blackcurrant 'Ebony' (*Ribes nigrum*)

This is the sweetest variety and can be eaten straight from the bush. The leaves are also edible but not that tasty. Height and spread 1m.

Rosemary (*Salvia rosmarinus*)

Whilst this plant is edible and used often in cooking, it can be toxic if consumed in large quantities so it's fine for nibbling on a few leaves; with its pungent aroma and strong flavour, it is unlikely a child would eat much, but it's one to keep an eye on.

Kale Daubenton 'Panache' (*Brassica oleracea ramosa*)

This kale has attractive variegated leaves. Every part is edible and my youngest child loved to bite the leaves straight from the plant, with no hands. Height 60cm, spread 1m.

Chives make a very pretty edge to a border or food forest corner

Swiss mint (*Mentha x piperita*)

Any type of mint can be substituted. Apple mint is nice for children as its leaves are soft and furry and are very tactile.

Babington's leek (*Allium ampeloprasum babingtonii*)

This is a perennial version of our traditional leek. The flower heads are a fun addition to a forest garden and children love to pull apart the heads into tiny bulbils. The bulbils are edible but are as strong as raw garlic so unlikely to be eaten by children. Leaves are harvested between January and March. Height 75cm, spread 10cm.

Chives (*Allium schoenoprasum*)

The leaves and flowers are edible and the chive is mild enough that they may be nibbled on a regular basis.

Daylily (*Hemerocallis fulva*)

All parts are edible but the main part that is eaten are the flowers and flower buds. Not to be confused with other lilies (*Lilium* sp.) which are toxic if eaten. They are a great flower to snack on in the garden.

Golden marjoram (*Origanum vulgare* 'Aureum')

You could use any oregano but this one is bright and colourful. I like to use the leaves in salads and the whole plant releases a wonderful aroma if brushed against or trampled on.

Bugle (*Ajuga reptans*)

This provides a very effective ground cover. The leaves and flowers are edible but not that tasty. They are good at recovering from some trampling by small feet.

Siberian bellflower (*Campanula poscharskyana*)

This bellflower forms a carpet of edible leaves. The purple flowers are also edible. Height 30cm, spread indefinite.

Violet 'Freckles' (*Viola sororia*)

This has beautiful dainty flowers. My daughter loved to carefully pick these to top cupcakes when going through a baking phase. The leaves are also edible and can be used in salads.

The soft leaves of apple mint are very tactile and have a milder mint flavour

Alpine strawberry 'Yellow Wonder' (*Fragaria vesca*)

This wild strawberry forms a clump rather than spreading by runners. It fruits well from spring until the first frosts but tends to slow down in the heat of mid-summer when it prefers some shade. Height and spread 25cm.

Oca (*Oxalis tuberosa*)

The main edible part is the root tuber but the flower and leaves are also edible so there is no worry about toxicity. They are bright and shiny and jewel-like when dug up, even before they have been washed so are a great crop to impress children.

Peas (*Pisum sativum*)

No garden for children would be complete without peas to eat straight from the pod. For the pea wigwam, grow a combination of two peas. A short one such as 'Jumbo' which grows to 75cm tall and provides peapods at an easy picking height, and a taller one such as 'Champion of England' which can grow up to 1.8m and will cover the wigwam structure and also provide some delicious peas.

You don't need to buy an acre of land to grow a forest garden.

Over a decade ago I did my Permaculture Design Certificate at the University of Bradford. Our final design project was to help produce a design for the newly started Horton Community Farm, just down the road. I had previously done a year long apprenticeship at RHS Harlow Carr. Whilst there, they had a demonstration plot measuring 3 x 3m to show how many vegetables you could grow in your own garden without the need for an allotment. This inspired my 3 x 3m forest garden design for Horton Community Farm.

The Mini Forest Garden

Scale 1:20

My original forest garden design for Horton community farm in 2011

3m x 3m FOREST GARDEN
PDC 2011 Synergy

I had done some experiments with perennial polycultures but it was all still pretty new to me. I decided wall-trained fruit would mean more sunlight could reach the ground and yields per square metre could be increased. Unlike the RHS annual vegetable plot, there would be other yields such as soil building, habitat for wildlife and the propagation of plants to be passed on to the community. I have always liked this design, even if it was never actually built at the farm. Recently whilst writing my book I felt it was time for a bit of tweaking and a few improvements. When I first approached this design I was a professional gardener with a little knowledge of permaculture and forest gardening. Over a decade later I am a professional forest gardener, and in permaculture design it is always so valuable, when tweaking a design, to reflect on what you have learnt in the process.

My first adventures in forest gardening were in my parents' field which had previously been grazed by sheep for probably hundreds of years. This field is still a very wild place where food yields are quite low in comparison to an annual vegetable plot but it takes almost no maintenance, still produces food and the wildlife is abundant compared to its previous history as short grazed grass. Over the last few years I have become much more interested and excited by the prospect of forest gardening in small spaces. I developed really successful forest garden beds in our yard at our previous home, which are between six and ten square metres in area. These are higher maintenance than our wild forest garden patches but nowhere near the intensity of annual vegetables. Part of my learning has been about purposely leaving gaps for annuals. Plants such as climbing beans and courgettes are very high yielding for the small space they occupy, so my designs are no longer exclusively perennial plants.

I have always grown my own food where possible but my professional background was in ornamental horticulture. When I first learnt about forest gardening, I decided I had to leave all that behind and only include plants that were edible, accumulated nutrients or were medicinal. Ten years on, I can see the importance of beauty in our forest gardens. If more people are to adopt this powerful way of growing their own food whilst providing space for nature, they have to be beautiful places to enjoy. I now design forest gardens filled with colour and interest all year round. Upright plants such as *Camassia*, *Iris* and *Crocosmia* can grow amongst the edibles, using the vertical space. Spring bulbs such

A combination that developed by accident in my yard forest garden includes the zesty golden oregano and umbellifer *Smyrium perfoiliatum*

Clear labels make identification easy for volunteers and visitors and also to remind yourself as you are learning. Here I have used willow and shaved off the bark to make a flat surface for writing on.

as crocus, dwarf narcissi and muscari come up early providing colour and nectar early on before dying back as other perennials take their place. When selecting plants, and there are always so many options, I now use aesthetics as one of the deciding factors.

A forest garden will provide much more habitat for wildlife than a lawn but the range of habitats is still limited so I now include stone piles and stacks of logs. You can build an insect hotel if you want to make a feature of habitats although recently I have learnt that it is best to make lots of small habitat boxes and space them around the garden to prevent diseases spreading. I have created sculptural stone piles in spiral shapes, still a great habitat but also adding an artistic feature to the garden. We should never underestimate the importance of fun in gardening. If we enjoy spending time in our forest garden, we are more likely to maintain it and notice when crops are ready to harvest. Friends and neighbours may be inspired and the forest garden network expands.

This stone spiral provides habitat and a way to creatively make use of the stones I keep digging out of the ground when I am planting things

Our climate is changing and we are suffering longer periods of drought than in the past. Water in the garden is becoming more important if we want to help wildlife survive these dry spells. I always include plenty of pollinator plants but sources of water are just as vital. This can be in the form of a small pond, a birdbath or even a shallow dish of water with pebbles in. Adding rocks to your water feature is important as many insects and bees cannot land on water without drowning and prefer to drink from the water's edge. I always include a pebbly 'beach' along one edge of a pond and a branch leaning into the water for other mammals to escape.

I will be honest and confess that there are many edible perennial plants that I find really unpalatable. My tastes have adapted over time but I still can't eat salad burnet (*Sanguisorba minor*) without grimacing. I have tended, over time, to use more and more traditional herbs and perennial vegetables. It is important to experiment so I like to include a couple of plants I haven't tried before. This year I am trying Korean aster (*Doellingeria scabra*) for the first time. A garden full of novelty plants that are technically edible but you are unlikely to eat is not much use.

Using the vertical is even more important in small spaces. If you like to grow a lot of salads, it can be hard to grow smaller, more tender plants, such as lettuce and basil, amongst your perennials which are likely to swamp them out. Some plants are also more prone to slug attacks. I have used a few green wall systems over the last few years and found them very useful for growing these more delicate plants. One pallet planter can provide more salads than we can eat, taking up only a very small amount of bed space in the garden. (See pallet planter design, p.83.)

Obelisks and archways provide more vertical growing opportunities and allow climbers to be grown where there are no large trees to use as a framework. I have included climbing beans, either French or runner beans, as they are very attractive, high yielding and fix nitrogen in the soil. Having managed a few community gardens over the years I now realise the importance of labelling plants, especially unusual ones. This gives confidence to everybody that they have the right plant and helps to build plant identification knowledge. My original design includes raised edges but now I use either flat or mounded beds as raised edges always dry out faster, requiring more inputs of time and water to keep plants hydrated. Wooden planks as edges make fantastic homes for slugs, with plants at the edges suffering more slug damage than others.

In a small space, creating a 'green wall' helps to make the most of the vertical

Overview of my learning

- Make space for annuals. This can really increase your yields and leave room for trying new things.
- Don't forget aesthetics. Make your garden beautiful and you will spend more time in it.
- Provide different habitats for wildlife. Include log or stone piles, bird boxes and bug hotels.
- Extend the season for pollinators using bulbs for early pollen and nectar sources.
- Grow things that will actually be eaten, but experiment too; that is where the best learning happens.
- Use the vertical. Grow on walls and up arches and obelisks.

Notes and scribbles when working out the layout for the updated version of the garden

Updated version of the garden

I have completed my diploma in applied permaculture design since my first mini forest garden design. My knowledge of permaculture design and practice has grown every year. I could never have imagined when sketching this first design and getting excited about forest gardening, that one day I would be working in, or designing a forest garden of some kind almost every day. The saying goes, you can never learn all there is to know about gardening and this is also true of permaculture. There is learning in every project I undertake. I like the idea of revisiting this design again in another 10 years and reflecting on what more I have learnt. The reality is, when you manage a forest garden, you are making tweaks all the time. Things die off, you replace them, other plants mature and spread out. Your needs change over time and so does your forest garden.

I have moved house and have a new garden. It had overgrown hedges and not much else, having not been maintained for around a decade. I am looking forward to the challenge of applying everything I have learnt over the years to design a small scale forest garden as part of an average sized suburban garden. I will no doubt tweak it many times following the triumphs and the failures. A garden is never finished, it is always evolving, as am I.

Plant list

Listed in layer order

Fig 'Brown Turkey' (*Ficus caria*)

This variety is very hardy down to -10°C. It fruits best when trained against a south-facing wall and with some root restriction, such as lining the planting hole with slabs. This is because in rich soil, the fig concentrates on leafy growth rather than producing fruit. Figs need full sun and prefer a stony, well-drained soil. The fruit ripens in late summer into autumn. 'Brunswick' is even hardier down to -12°C but fruits later in September to October so there is the risk the fruit may be damaged by an early frost.

Kale 'Daubentons' (*Brassica oleracea ramosa*)

This perennial kale grows into a small shrub around 1m tall. In this small space, branches are given some support as it can grow to 1m high but has a tendency for the branches to flop down and crush other plants. It is evergreen so you can harvest the leaves year round.

Raspberry 'Ruby Beauty' (*Rubus idaeus*)

This is a high yielding, compact cultivar growing to just 1m in height meaning you can fit several plants in a small space. I plant them in a circle and tie the canes together at the top but you may wish to add some support for individual canes as this variety is quite branching compared to most raspberries. The fruits are lovely and sweet.

Japanese quince (*Chaenomeles japonica*)

This thorny, deciduous shrub has stunning bright red, pink, orange or white flowers in spring and fragrant fruit in the autumn. The fruit makes a very fragrant, zesty jam but is very tart and bitter when raw. The small, hard fruit smell amazing and we often have a bowl of fruit in the house in winter to fill the room with their lemony floral scent. The fruit are very high in pectin so are useful for jam and jelly making. I mix them with apples to make fruit leather. They are easy to grow against a wall or fence and can grow up to 2.5m tall but can be pruned to be quite narrow, around 40cm. They tolerate a wide range of soil including heavy clay soil.

Redcurrant 'Rovada' (*Ribes rubrum*)

To fit in a small space, redcurrants can be wall trained. 'Rovada' is a heavy cropping cultivar with large fruit which ripen in late summer. The main issue is getting to them before the birds do. Redcurrants are shade tolerant so you could grow a tall crop in front of them to hide them from the birds. I have done this successfully using nettles before but you won't want to let nettles loose in such a small garden. In this design I have used salsify to provide some protection.

Purple sage (*Saliva officinalis 'Purpurascens'*)

This sub-shrub is evergreen with beautiful purple/grey leaves which give a contrast against all the other green leaves around it. It needs full sun and a well-drained spot. It will rot if the ground stays wet over winter. It is a small shrub reaching around 50cm in height.

Welsh onion (*Allium fistulosum*)

This is a bulbous perennial also known as Japanese bunching onion. You can harvest the hollow stems year round and also harvest the bulbs. They can be used in a similar way to spring onions and have a mild onion flavour.

Korean aster (*Doellingeria scabra*)

This is my experiment this year so I haven't eaten it yet but it has been growing in my garden and I can say the white, daisy-like flowers are very pretty. It is a herbaceous perennial that is very popular in Korea as a spring vegetable. The young leaves can be eaten raw or cooked and the older leaves are traditionally picked and dried. These dried leaves are then rehydrated and added to stir-fry or eaten on their own as a green vegetable. I will reserve judgement until I have tried these myself but it is always good to try something new.

Apple mint (*Mentha suaveolens*)

A milder flavoured mint than spearmint or peppermint that can be added to salads, fruit salads and mint jelly. It has attractive hairy leaves and the flowers are loved by pollinators.

Garlic chives (*Allium tuberosum*)

This allium is used as a herb. The bulb is too fibrous to eat so cut the leaves as you would normal chives. It has long thin and flattened leaves that taste mildly of garlic. The pretty white, star-shaped flowers bloom in July and August and are lovely in salads or sprinkled on stir-fries. They like a moist soil in a sunny position.

Salsify (*Tragopogon porrifolius*)

Salsify used to be commonly grown but fell out of favour in recent times. It is grown predominantly for its root which can be eaten grated raw into salads or cooked as you would any root vegetable. It is said to taste like oysters but as I haven't eaten oysters I can't say if I agree. The flowering shoots and young leaves are also edible raw or cooked. Flowering starts in June and lasts until August. The seeds ripen in late summer and can be sprouted and added to salads. The seed heads are beautiful and add interest to the border. It is a biennial but my experience is that it self-seeds prolifically so shouldn't need replanting. It will grow in most soils, even heavy clay soil but needs a sunny spot.

Grecian bellflower (*Campanula versicolor*)

This is the tastiest of all campanulas and can be used in large quantities in salads. The leaves are rich in vitamin C and are usually available year round. The flowers are also sweet. If you live in a cold area and *C. versicolor* doesn't survive, you could try *C. persicifolia* which is hardier. It also has leaves year round and they are still tasty but they are quite long and thin so a bit more fiddly to harvest. I have also found it to be a bit more shade tolerant than *C. versicolor.*

Daylily 'Stella de Oro' (*Hemerocallis* sp.)

At just 30-50cm tall, this daylily is perfect for smaller gardens. It has fragrant yellow flowers in summer which can be eaten raw in salads and the buds can be added to stir-fries.

Lemon balm (*Melissa officinalis*)

The strong scent of the leaves makes this an effective pest confuser, protecting your crops from pest damage. The flowers are also useful at attracting beneficial insects. The leaves have powerful medicinal qualities and can be made into a tea and also added to salads and as a flavouring in other dishes. It is a fairly vigorous plant and grows happily in most soils but does not like too much shade or waterlogged soils.

Courgette 'Gold Rush' (*Cucurbita pepo*)

You could use any courgette here. I chose 'Gold Rush' because I love the flavour and look of the bright yellow fruit. It is also nice and compact, forming a bush rather than trailing. Cougette can be started under glass or on a windowsill and planted out in late May once all risk of frost is over.

Hosta 'Blue angel' (*Hosta sieboldiana*)

This hosta is a vigorous plant, meaning it is more able to deal with slugs and being harvested. You eat the young

Bees love the flowers of Welsh onion so although they are edible, I leave them for the wildlife to enjoy

This salsify self-seeded into this spot. The flowers are very pretty so I leave it in so long as it is not swamping out other plants.

Sweet violet looks so delicate but is actually quite tough and can cope with drought and shade

leaf shoots in stir-fries. It produces a pale purple flower on a tall flower spike in mid summer which is also edible. Other hostas are also edible but not all are tasty. This one grows to a height of 75cm and spread of around 0.5-1m.

Sea holly 'Jos Eijking' (*Eryngium* x *zabelii*)

The stems and flowers of this plant are a striking bright blue. It is loved by pollinators, and spiders often make webs between its foliage as the stems are so stiff and strong. It needs full sun and good drainage.

Achillea 'Moonshine'

The flowers, much loved by pollinators, are a bright lemon yellow and bloom from late spring right up to early autumn. The upright stems grow to a height of 60cm. *Achillea* needs full sun and a moist but well-drained soil.

Sweet violet (*Viola odorata*)

The leaves are edible in salads and are usually available all year round so a valuable winter salad plant. It is a useful ground cover plant reaching a height of just 10cm. The flowers of sweet violet are often candied and used to decorate cakes and puddings.

Alpine strawberry (*Fragaria vesca*)

These tiny strawberries are so tough they make a great ground cover. The fruits may be small but they are packed with flavour. The flowers and leaves can also be eaten in salads or brewed into a tea. I tend to use this strawberry in preference to the larger cultivated strawberry because it is so disease resistant. They can become invasive if not managed properly which is fine in a wilder setting but in a small garden such as this, they just need pulling up when they start to outcompete their neighbouring plants.

Bugle (*Ajuga reptans*)

One of my most used ground covers as it is so pretty, bugle covers the ground to suppress weeds and attracts bees with its purple/blue flowers in spring. The leaves are edible but I don't enjoy eating them so plant it for the other functions it provides.

Golden marjoram 'Aurea' (*Oreganum vulgare*)

This attractive woody perennial is an effective ground cover plant forming a dense mat of zesty yellow/green foliage up to 30cm tall. The aromatic leaves can be used fresh or dried and added to mixed herbs. I enjoy adding small amounts to salads to add colour and flavour. The pale pink flowers are also edible and available in late summer. It prefers full sun but can tolerate some shade. It can rot in wet soils so ideally choose a well-drained site.

Thyme 'Silver Queen' (*Thymus* sp.)

Thyme is technically a dwarf shrub but it functions as a ground cover so I have added it here. 'Silver Queen' is evergreen and grows to just 30cm in height and spread. Its leaves are lemon scented and edged white making it an attractive addition to the planting scheme. It has tiny pale pink flowers in summer which are also edible. It needs full sun and good drainage and won't tolerate any competition from other plants.

Camas (*Camassia quamash*)

The flower spikes of star-shaped blue flowers, appearing in May/June, can reach up to 80cm in height but are often much shorter. It is a bulb and prefers moist soil in part shade or full sun. The bulb is edible when cooked but needs a long cooking time. It can be baked then dried and ground into a powder for thickening soups or mixed with flour for baking.

Hooker's onion (*Allium hookeri*)

This bulbous perennial is eaten as you would chives. The creamy white flowers are very attractive to pollinators and are also edible and lovely in salads. It is bigger than chive, growing to a height of up to 60cm although mine is usually closer to 40cm.

Chinese artichoke (*Stachys affinis*)

The tubers of Chinese artichoke are quite small but are still a valuable crop to grow. They add some nice crunch to a stir-fry similar to water chestnuts. In Japan it is often pickled which is something I am hoping to try this year. The leaves are quite attractive, soft and fuzzy with purple flowers in late summer. It is not too fussy about soil type although I have had poor harvests in heavy soil and in poor soil so I like to add a good amount of mulch each year to enrich the soil. It doesn't mind a bit of shade but does not like too much competition from other plants.

Saffron (*Crocus sativus*)

This expensive spice is used around the world to add a distinctive flavour and yellow colour to food. The corm is planted in autumn and it flowers the following autumn. When flowering, the styles and stigmas are harvested and dried to store for later use. It grows to just 10cm tall, needs full sun and likes free draining soils.

Honeysuckle 'Sweet Sue' (*Lonicera periclymenum*)

'Sweet Sue' is a fairly compact honeysuckle at around 2.4m in height, perfect for smaller gardens. The flowers are edible and can be used to make syrups, cordials and tea or simply added to salads or fruit salads.

My forest garden designs have become much more beautiful over time. There are so many edible flowers that are are also great for pollinators.

Food Forest Border

If you thought the 3m x 3m food forest was as small as it gets, think again.

In spring 2023, I entered a design for a micro show garden at the Harrogate spring flower show in North Yorkshire. My aim was simply to create a tiny version of a food forest in a raised bed border to demonstrate to visitors the concepts of a multilayered edible garden and encourage them to grow one at home. The size was 1.2m x 3.6m, just over four square metres. The show attracts over 40,000 visitors each year so what better way to spread the word about permaculture and food forests than to have a living example to show people?

The original border design I submitted to the flower show

Even in the tiny space available, I wanted to include all the learning from redesigning the 3m x 3m design, so I included a dead hedge as the central sculptural feature and used an old tin planter as a pond. Materials were gathered from across all the gardens I manage. I enjoyed many hours of 'foraging' and filling baskets and wheelbarrows with pine cones, sticks covered in lichen and old rotting logs.

The border was designed as a mini ecosystem, including edible crops, nutrient cycling plants, nitrogen fixers and wildlife habitat. As the show was in the spring, I chose spring-flowering plants and foliage plants with contrasting leaf colours to add interest and depth to the planting design. The small pond provided water for birds and insects and reflected the surrounding planting, adding a sense of calm. Hazel poles held together a dead hedge in a wave like shape, giving height but without casting shade. At the base of the wave I used twigs to create the dead hedge; a band of habitat, hiding places and hollows for small garden creatures to thrive. Hazel plant labels shared the name of the plant and whether it was edible or had some other use in the garden.

I chose a colour scheme of purples, blues and white as I felt it would look fresh for spring but also rich in colour. The show is in April each year and, especially in the north of England, this really restricted my plant choices. Here I have tweaked the design a bit as show gardens are not representative of real life; everything needs to be in full bloom for that exact date. For this reason I have added plants that flower in summer and autumn too for the benefit of pollinators but also to make it more attractive year round.

An important element to the garden was the wildlife habitat. Even in such a small space I managed to fit both a stone and log pile and I used dead wood and pine cones as a mulch to encourage decomposers and other soil life to thrive in the border. The best news is that we won top prize for best border at the show. I was very pleasantly surprised as I had assumed the judges would be looking for something more traditional. We all had a great discussion about permaculture and the design of food forests. The best feedback was that it was the first ever garden they had felt necessary to fact check as they didn't believe hostas were edible. Every day is a school day, even for flower show judges.

Tracing the shape of the dead hedge helped me to get the shape right for the space

We created the dead hedge feature using willow poles and a mix of willow and foraged twigs for the infill

Due to the nature of the show, I used pretty small trees – the design would have looked better with bigger trees. It was also a cold April day and no apples were in blossom at the time so I had to substitute a plum tree.

My labels which proved a teaching tool even for the judges

The dead hedge was a joy to forage for, really immersing myself in the tiny details such as moss and lichen on twigs

Plant list

Apple 'Red Devil' *(Malus domestica)*

This variety of apple has attractive pink flowers in the spring and red fruit in September making it highly attractive. It is self-fertile so does not need another tree to pollinate it, although yields are usually higher if you can provide a pollinator. The fruit also has some red in the flesh which produces a pink juice. The rootstock you choose when buying an apple tree determines its size. In this small space I chose rootstock M9 which would give an eventual height and spread of 2.5m. If you want something even smaller, M27 is extremely dwarfing giving an eventual height of 1.5-1.8m. Both will require fertile soil and supplementary water during prolonged dry periods to do well.

Blackcurrant 'Ben Sarek' *(Ribes nigrum)*

This is a really compact variety that will even grow well in containers, reaching a maximum height of around 1.2m. It has large berries with excellent flavour and its flowers are very frost resistant so it's a good variety for climates similar to the north of England. The fruit can be used both as a dessert berry and for culinary use. (See jam guild design p.50, for more details.)

Sage 'Tricolor' *(Salvia officinalis)*

This sage is evergreen and its leaves are variegated with splashes of pink on the leaves. It is a very attractive alternative to the green sage. It is a Mediterranean herb so it likes full sun and a well-drained soil. In my experience, if you have clay soil you are better growing it in a container as it will rot if the soil is waterlogged over winter. It produces purple/blue flowers in summer and leaves can be harvested year round. The height and spread are 0.5m-1m.

Perennial kale Daubentons 'Panache' *(Brassica oleracea* var. *ramosa)*

This perennial kale is very ornamental with its variegated leaves. It is not as large as some, with a height and spread of around 1m but it does have a tendency for its branches to flop down onto the ground. It is evergreen so can be harvested year round. Its leaves are more tender in summer so can be used in salads but in winter it is more suitable for steaming or in stews. It will grow in most soils but doesn't like to dry out or to sit in waterlogged soils where it may rot over winter.

Mahonia 'Winter Sun' *(Mahonia x media)*

This cultivar flowers all winter from November until February providing a valuable source of pollen and nectar and a wonderful scent. It is grown for its berries. It can grow to 4m tall and wide but can be crown lifted (removing the lower branches) and trained to form a tall tower of foliage and flowers, leaving plenty of room for under planting. They prefer some shade and moist soil but are fairly tolerant of a wide range of conditions. (See tropical style food forest, p.74, for more details.)

Service berry *(Amelanchier canadensis)*

One of my favourite small trees, this can be kept quite small with yearly pruning. It is one of the first plants to fruit in the garden. It is particularly attractive thanks to its bronze buds in early spring followed by clouds of white flowers a few weeks later, its dark purple edible fruit in June then vivid autumn colour at the end of the year. If left unpruned it can reach 6m. It prefers a slightly acid to neutral, moist soil.

Gooseberry 'Invicta' *(Ribes uva-crispa)*

This is a high yielding but compact variety suitable for small gardens with a height and spread of 1m. It can be used as both a dessert and culinary berry.

Trailing rosemary 'Prostrata' *(Salvia rosmarinus)*

Using a trailing variety of rosemary in a raised bed means you can squeeze one into a very small space. Rosemary doesn't like competition from tall plants so give it plenty of light. (See first aid kit garden, p.88, for more details.)

Lemon balm *(Melissa officinalis)*

See mini forest garden design, p.34, for more details.

Good King Henry (*Blitum bonus-henricus*)

The leaves can be used as a spinach substitute. The stem can be eaten as asparagus and the flower buds can be cooked like broccoli. It has been eaten as a green vegetable for centuries. The leaves do get more bitter in the summer so are best eaten in spring. This is a very tough plant which will grow in most soils and positions but it prefers moist soil in part shade. The full grown stems reach a height of 75cm and a similar spread.

Lupin 'Gallery Yellow' (*Lupinus*)

This is a compact yellow lupin which is included for its ability to improve the fertility of the soil thanks to its nitrogen fixing nodules on its roots. It grows to a height of 50cm with a spread of 30cm, flowering May to July. Cutting off the flower spikes once they have bloomed will prolong the flowering period. It will grow happily in full sun and part shade and prefers a well-drained soil.

Hosta (*Hosta undulata* var. *undulata*)

This pretty variegated hosta has cream coloured leaves with a wide margin of green along the edges. The pale foliage really stands out in the shade. The young shoots are edible in salads or stir-fries. The flowers, blooming in summer, are pollen and nectar rich, attractive to pollinators and also edible. Hosta will grow well in full sun if the soil is always moist. They grow very well in part shade to full shade. This variety has a height of 45cm and a spread of 30cm.

Turkish rocket (*Bunius orientalis*)

I love this plant. Each year I look forward to seeing, smelling and eating its flowers. It has large long green leaves which can be eaten but I find them a little bitter, even more so in the summer months. I much prefer eating the flowering shoots, before the buds open, steamed like broccoli or the flowers themselves in summer. They are such a wonderful insect attractant plant that I have to gently shake off hoverflies when harvesting the flowers as they are constantly buzzing around it. If you keep harvesting the unopened flowering shoots, it will keep producing them for several weeks. If you want to eat both the shoots and the opened flowers, it is best to have two or more clumps so you can manage them differently. It has a long taproot which makes it able to access water even in drought conditions so will grow in most soils, even relatively dry ones if they are deep. It prefers a sunny site but will tolerate some shade.

Trailing rosemary mixed with *Campanula*, thyme, chives and *Camassia*

Siberian bellflower (*Campanula poscharskyana*)

This plant is a very useful winter salad leaf crop. It is a ground hugging mat-forming perennial which performs very well as a living mulch, leaving little bare soil for weed seeds to germinate. I have grown it in very shady spots under gooseberries and blackcurrants and it has grown very happily although it does flower better in sunnier spots. It is also very drought tolerant and can grow in the cracks in walls or pavements. The purple/blue star-shaped flowers are very tasty in salads and I often have a nibble on a few while gardening. It is a short plant with a height of just 10-15cm but with a much larger spread if given the space.

Alpine strawberry (*Fragaria vesca*)

See mini forest garden design, p.34, for more details.

Bugle 'Variegata' (*Ajuga reptans*)

This variety grows to around 15cm tall and forms a mat of green and white variegated foliage, helping to keep the soil moist and stopping weed seeds from germinating. It has purple/blue flowers from May to June.

Violet 'Freckles' (*Viola sororia*)

This has the most beautiful pale purple flowers with speckles of dark purple that look very dainty on top of a cupcake or topping a salad. The leaves are also edible in a salad and when cooked can thicken soups. It spreads in a dense low growing clump and is happy to grow in quite a bit of shade or in sunny spots although it doesn't like to be baked dry. It's a small plant at 15cm tall with a spread of 20cm although if it's happy, it will form a larger clump. It will grow in most soils but prefers a slightly acidic soil.

Oregano 'Variegata' (*Origanum vulgare*)

This is a fully hardy, perennial aromatic herb with green foliage that is edged with a white margin and produces small pink flowers. The leaves and flowers can be used in cooking as with any oregano. I like to add the fresh leaves to salads for a herby flavour. The flowers are very popular with pollinators so they can attract beneficial insects to your garden. It's quite low growing to 30cm but it spreads out to form wide clumps around 45-50cm wide. It tolerates most soils but will rot in heavy clay or waterlogged soil.

Lemon thyme (*Thymus citriodorus*)

This thyme can be used in herbal tea or for flavouring food. It is a bit too strong a flavour to use raw in salads. (See first aid kit garden, p.88, for more details.)

Wild hyacinth 'Caerulea' (*Camassia leichlinii*)

This plant is a bulb and is very easy to grow despite its exotic appearance. It produces stunning spires of blue flowers in April to May; it is one of my favourite plants. The bulb can be eaten roasted as a potato substitute, although it's much too pretty to eat in my opinion. *Camassia* are rich in pollen and nectar so loved by pollinators. The flower spikes can reach 0.9-1m with a spread of 40cm. They are fairly unfussy but prefer a well-drained moist soil. They are happy in a meadow, their natural habitat, and can be naturalised in turf and wild grassy areas.

Chinese artichokes (*Stachys affinis*)

These are tiny tubers which some say look like fat maggots. They have a flavour and texture a bit like water chestnuts but nuttier. They are brilliant in salads or stir-fried. They also have a pretty purple flower which you can leave for colour and interest or cut off if you are wanting to maximise yield of the tubers. The tubers are harvested from late October once the top growth has turned brown. Replant a few tubers to ensure more will grow the following year. They grow best in a moist but free draining, fertile soil without too much competition. On occasions I have allowed too many weeds to grow around them and the tubers were so tiny as to hardly be worth cooking. When happy they reach a height of 60cm. (See mini forest garden, p.34, for more details.)

I hope this design has demonstrated that you can grow edible perennial plants, even a food forest, in just a raised bed. Make sure if you are creating a raised bed straight onto a hard surface like tarmac or paving, rather than directly onto soil, that you provide a good depth of soil, at least 30cm, ideally more. This will also need additional watering in dry periods as the plant roots cannot go deep into the soil to find ground water.

Chinese artichoke start small but have delicious small edible tubers which you harvest as the plant dies down in late autumn

Jam Guild

Fresh berry fruit can be some of the most expensive fruit in the shops. This is partly due to the difficulty of picking, packing and transporting it.

Growing your own is probably the only cost effective way of making your own jam.

This guild (a selection of plants that work together to support one another) could have an apple as its keystone species but apples are relatively cheap to buy and it's much easier to find someone with a glut of apples than most other fruit. I have put a plum at the centre as they are such a delicious fruit to pick and eat, especially when still warm from the heat of the sun. Plum jam is also fabulous, especially when you find a jar deep in winter when fruit is a real treat. You could substitute the plum for a cherry or damson, both of which also make wonderful jam.

Gathering the plum harvest to make jam and fruit leather

I used to run a farmers' market stall selling foraged jams and jellies and we made many kinds of unusual flavour combinations such as 'fuchsia and pear drizzling sauce', 'mirabelle and elderflower jam' and 'lemon balm and crab apple jelly'. I love experimenting with adding herbs and other wild fruits in jams; just make small batches so if you don't like it, you haven't wasted too much fruit. If you don't have room for a bed of this shape and size in your garden, you could consider growing a jam hedge instead. I first came across the concept of a jam hedge while chatting with Alan from Fruit Works, a local cooperative who plant and maintain fruit trees and orchards in community and school gardens. What an excellent way to add fruit to your garden whilst also providing privacy, shelter, a place for birds to nest and forage opportunities if in a public space.

The jam guild planting plan. Your plan doesn't have to be to scale. It can be quite rough so long as it represents the right shape and size of your garden. I have used pencil lines to divide the bed into roughly 1m squares.

Plant list

Plum 'Jubilee' (*Prunus domestica*)

PRIMARY CROP, KEYSTONE SPECIES

A sweet dessert plum that is also self-fertile and is said to be superior to 'Victoria', with larger fruit and higher yields. If grown on a Pixy rootstock, which is semi-dwarfing, the eventual height and spread is 2-2.5m meaning it won't cast too much shade. Fruit is harvested in early autumn and can be eaten straight off the tree, made into jam or simply bottled.

The gooseberry 'Hinnomaki red' has beautiful fruit and are easier to harvest than green ones because you can see them better

Gooseberry 'Hinnomaki Red' (*Ribes uva-crispa*)

SECONDARY CROP, ATTRACTOR PLANT

This is an easy to grow, vigorous red gooseberry with an upright habit and great disease resistance. They grow to a height of 1.5m and a spread of 0.5-1m so perfect for using the vertical space and leaving plenty of room for under planting. They prefer a moist but not waterlogged, fertile soil but they will grow in most soils. Gooseberries are very shade tolerant so are ideal for planting under trees in part shade and will even tolerate almost full shade.

This elder has the most delicate leaves and the dark coloured foliage gives a striking contrast to the other green leaves

Elderflower 'Black Lace' (*Sambucus nigra*)

SECONDARY CROP, ATTRACTOR PLANT

You can add elderberries to fruit jam but I also use the flowers to add a very floral note. 'Black Lace' has beautiful dark purple/black leaves which add much needed colour in a garden mostly full of green foliage. The flowers appear in May to June and the fruit ripen in August to September. Elder prefers a slightly acidic and moist soil and will grow in semi-shade but flower and fruit best where it gets the most sun. It makes a great addition to a mixed hedge.

Crab apple (*Malus sylvestris*)

SECONDARY CROP, ATTRACTOR PLANT

When grown as a very dwarf tree on rootstock M26, it can be pruned as a minarette, a columnar shaped tree meaning you can fit it into a very small garden. Crab apples also make a great hedge or addition to a mixed hedge. If you have the space, they make a lovely small tree in the garden. *M. sylvestris* 'Evereste' is very floriferous and bears orange fruit. Its leaves turn lovely shades of yellow and orange in the autumn. *M. sylvestris* 'Golden Hornet' has a very long flowering period, covering most of the periods other apples are in flower, so is a great pollinator for other apple varieties. It has beautiful golden yellow fruits that are great for jams and jellies.

Blackcurrant 'Ben Hope' (*Ribes nigrum*)

SECONDARY CROP, ATTRACTOR PLANT

This variety has an upright habit leaving more space for under planting. It has good pest and disease

The red hairs on the wineberry stems make it look like it is glowing

Rosa spinossisima also makes lovely jam and its black hips make a pink jam

resistance which is always helpful in an organic setting. The fruit ripens from July into early August. The shrub has a height and spread of 1.5m and you can remove some of the lower branches if you want to give more light to the under planting. Blackcurrants fruit best in the sun but will tolerate some shade. They are not fussy about soil but will grow best in moist but well-drained fertile soil. 'Ben Connan' and 'Titania' are also compact varieties suitable for smaller gardens.

Wineberry (*Rubus phoenicolasius*)

SECONDARY CROP, ATTRACTOR PLANT
This rubus has very attractive stems covered in tiny red spines and in autumn the leaves turn a lovely yellow colour before they fall. It is quite a large plant growing up to 2m and spreading up to 4m so one to keep trained if you have limited space. It fruits in late summer producing small very tasty orange red fruits. It will grow happily in most soils but prefers a well-drained moist soil and a sunny position.

Raspberry (*Rubus idaeus*)

SECONDARY CROP, ATTRACTOR PLANT
There are so many cultivars to choose from and if you want a long season of cropping, grow both summer and autumn fruiting canes. For summer, one of the best varieties 'Malling Jewel' produces large, juicy, sweet fruit early in the season. For autumn, I love the yellow fruiting 'All Gold' as the birds tend not to eat them as quickly, maybe they don't realise they are ripe – they are delicious.

Japanese rose (*Rosa rugosa*)

SECONDARY CROP, ATTRACTOR PLANT
You can make jams and syrups from any rosehip but this rose produces large, fleshy and sweet hips from late summer onwards. The deep pink flowers have a beautiful scent and the petals can also be used to flavour jams and jellies. The glossy green leaves turn a lovely shade of yellow in autumn. *Rosa rugosa* is a very tough, disease resistant rose that will grow almost anywhere.

Rhubarb 'Glaskins Perpetual' (*Rheum x hybridum*)

SECONDARY CROP, MULCHER

This heritage rhubarb is so valuable as it can be picked from late spring, right up to the start of autumn. It has very low levels of oxalic acid which don't increase as you move into summer, as happens with other rhubarbs. The heavy cropping stems are green with a flush of red and are lovely and sweet.

Strawberry 'Buddy' (*Fragaria x ananassa*)

SECONDARY CROP, SUPPRESSOR PLANT

There are so many different types of strawberries you can select for crops at different times of the year. You could choose from those that fruit early (mid-June – early July), mid-season (late June to mid-July) or late season (throughout July). 'Buddy' is an everbearing variety that produces fruit all through the summer until the first frosts. If you only have a small area available for strawberries you may want to have a crop that all ripen in one season to produce enough to make jam. 'Buddy' is one of the most heavy cropping and disease resistant everbearing strawberries but the crop will be spread out over the season. I usually choose alpine strawberries in my own garden as they are so tough but it would take forever to harvest enough to make even one jar of jam; believe me, I've tried.

Apple mint (*Mentha suaveolens*) and/or spearmint (*Mentha spicata*)

CONFUSER PLANT

Also known as garden mint, spearmint is the most commonly used mint when making mint jelly but many prefer a milder flavour such as apple mint. Both are pretty tough plants that will grow in most soils. It is best to plant mint with a barrier around it to stop it taking over your beds. Personally I love the punch of spearmint in my mint jelly.

Lemon balm (*Melissa officinalis*)

CONFUSER PLANT

I have used lemon balm leaves to flavour jellies and it gives a beautiful refreshing tang to a delicate jelly made with crab apples. It is a tough plant and will grow in most soils but it does prefer some sun although it will tolerate shade.

The leaves and seeds of sweet cicely can be used to add a sweetness to jams

Sweet cicely (*Myrrhis odorata*)

ATTRACTOR PLANT

This is a brilliant plant for the shadier spots in the guild as it prefers dappled shade. Sweet cicely leaves and seed pods are used to sweeten fruit, especially rhubarb, when making crumbles, sorbets and fruit salads and add an aniseed note. I have not used it for making jellies but it is primarily used in conjunction with fruit so I thought I would add it to this guild as it is also useful for attracting beneficial insects for pest control.

Lupin (*Lupinus* sp.)

NITROGEN FIXER

These have been added for their nitrogen fixing properties. You can get both annual and perennial lupins. I prefer the perennial lupins as they come back each year with no added input from me. Some people struggle to grow lupins due to slug damage and lupin aphid. When you start to use ecological gardening practices,

Gooseberry and elderflower jam

A favourite in my household is gooseberry and elderflower jam but often the flowers are over before the gooseberries are ripe so we pick the flowers, separate the flowers from the stems using a fork and add them to a tub with just enough water to cover and a squeeze of lemon juice and freeze them.

Elderflowers should be removed from the green stalks to prevent bitter flavours. I like to store some in a tupperware by freezing them in a block of ice.

Ingredients

6 heads of elderflowers, removed from the stalks
500g gooseberries
500g sugar
200ml water (if using frozen flowers, count the water towards the total)
4 tbsp lemon juice

1. Sterilise your jars in the oven at 120°C for 15 min and place a plate into the freezer (this is for testing the setting point of the jam).

2. Place the gooseberries, water and lemon juice into a large pan, ideally a wide jam pan and bring to the boil. Turn the heat down and simmer for 15-20 minutes until the fruit has softened.

3. Add the sugar and stir until the sugar is dissolved, keeping the heat low, this should be around 10-15 minutes. Once all the sugar has dissolved, turn up the heat and boil rapidly for 10 minutes. Foamy 'scum' will form on the surface, skim this off as it boils.

4. Take your chilled plate and drop a small amount of jam onto the plate. Push your finger into the blob of jam, if it wrinkles, the jam is ready to put in jars. If not, keep boiling for a few more minutes and try again. When ready, pour the jam into jars and put the lid on immediately.

You can use this basic recipe for any fruit. Gooseberries are high in pectin so you can use ordinary granulated sugar. If your fruit is not high in pectin, you can use a jam sugar which has pectin added. If the jam still doesn't set, rebrand it as a drizzling sauce. This is what I used to do for the farmers' market stall. Great to drizzle on yogurt, icecream or pancakes.

building up soil life, creating habitat for creatures who eat slugs, then damage is much reduced. As for the aphids, keep an eye out and blast them off with water at the first sight of them. With any luck, something else in the garden may get a taste for them and control them for you. If you still struggle with pests, remove the lupins from the design and add in more of the other nitrogen fixers. If your soil is rich and high in nitrogen then add more plants for pollinators.

Creeping comfrey 'Hidcote Blue' (*Symphytum*)

SUPPRESSOR PLANT, MULCHER

I use this ground cover comfrey quite a lot as it is only 45cm tall, not the huge beast that is 'Bocking 14'. It will grow happily in the shadiest parts of the guild acting as a dynamic accumulator and its leaves can be cut and used as a mulch for the crop plants in the guild.

Everlasting pea (*Lathyrus latifolius*)

NITROGEN FIXER

This is another nitrogen fixing plant which is also great for pollinators. It is a sprawling, perennial climber growing up to 2m so is best grown up a support to prevent it swamping out neighbouring plants. It is happy in most soils and any position other than deep shade.

Bistort 'Superba' (*Bistorta officinalis*)

ATTRACTOR PLANT, SUPPRESSOR PLANT

This is an ingredient in 'dock pudding' (oatmeal, nettles, onions and bacon) and flowers from June to September to a height of 75cm. The leaves and young shoots are eaten in spring ideally before flowering. The leaves are a bit like spinach but fairly bland so more of an addition to other ingredients. It prefers a moist to wet soil and can grow in a wide range of soils, even a very acid soil. This is in this design as a ground cover and pollinator plant that tolerates shade. It can be invasive in a sunny position but tends to behave better in shadier spots.

Lavender 'Hidcote' (*Lavandula angustifolia*)

CONFUSER PLANT

There are a few types of lavender, each with a different flavour but I prefer the *angustifolia* ones which flower from mid-summer until the end of July, occasionally having a second flush of flowers. *Lavandula* x *intermedia* are larger shrubs and flower later, from July until the end of August. I don't feel I need both in terms of a long harvesting season as it is very easy to dry lavender flowers to use later in the year. The flowers make a wonderful addition to scones to be eaten with lashings of cream and strawberry jam. You can also use the flowers to make a floral jelly with crab apples.

Herbs such as lavender and lemon verbena can be used to add flavour to jams and jellies. These herbs can be picked and dried but I prefer to use them fresh.

Bulbs

I have added bulbs for colour in spring and to provide a food source for pollinators when not much is flowering. I have selected dwarf daffodil 'Hawera' (*Narcissus* sp.), *Muscari armenicum, Crocus* 'Pickwick' and perennial dwarf tulip 'Everlasting Mixed' (*Tulipa* sp.) but make your own selections based on your colour preferences.

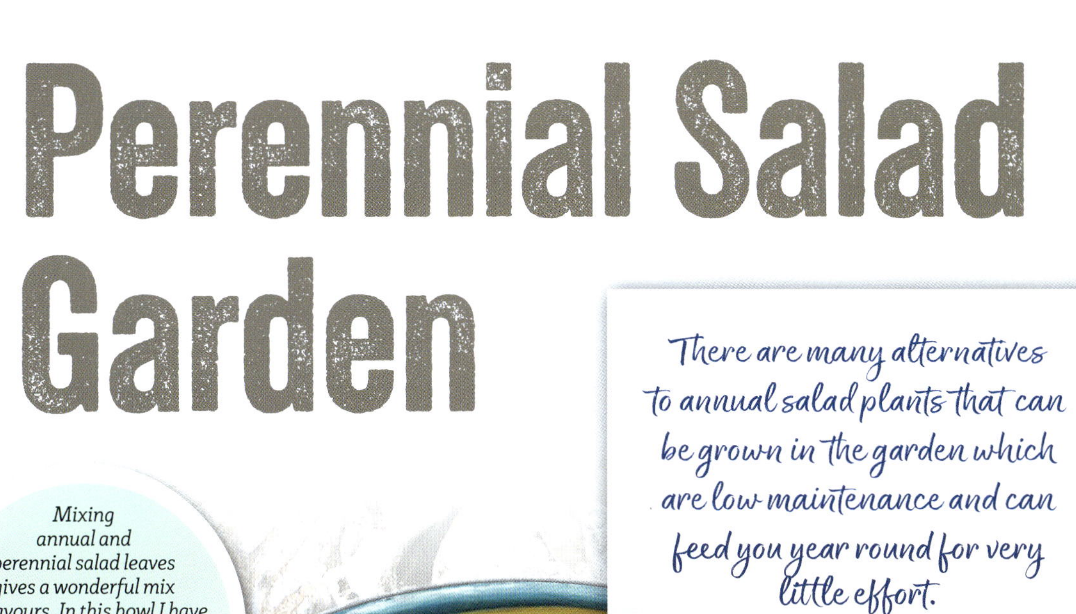

Perennial Salad Garden

There are many alternatives to annual salad plants that can be grown in the garden which are low maintenance and can feed you year round for very little effort.

*Mixing annual and perennial salad leaves gives a wonderful mix of flavours. In this bowl I have picked Chinese mallow (*Malva crispa*), buck's horn plantain, nasturtium, caucasian spinach, golden oregano, mountain spinach and mizuna.*

Salad leaves are one of the easiest crops to grow at home. You can grow salad in a window box or even indoors on a windowsill. Pea shoots and microgreens (the young seedlings) of herbs and brassicas are other popular salad crops that can be grown indoors through the winter too. The only downside to salad crops is that they need to be sown every few weeks then watered and monitored carefully to keep them growing well. There are many alternatives to annual salad plants that can be grown in the garden which are low maintenance and can feed you year round for very little effort. They each have a distinctive taste and it can take a while to adjust to a salad that has more flavour. You could start by introducing a few leaves into your regular salads to see if you like the taste. Then add more and more of the alternative crops until you find you don't need to buy salad anymore. It is also absolutely fine if you cannot get used to a flavour so leave it out. I still cannot find a way to enjoy salad burnet, but I do occasionally give it another try, just in case.

Sorrel grows well even in the shade, giving a very strong tasting flavour to a salad or stir-fry

Plant list

Salad burnet (*Sanguisorba minor*)

This has very pretty leaves that have a hint of cucumber about them. Best picked when young and tender. They like full sun or part shade and prefer an alkaline soil. They grow to a height of 60cm and a spread of 30cm.

Oxeye daisy (*Leucanthemum vulgare*)

These wildflowers vary in bitterness; some can be delicious, some not, so try a leaf before you pick too much. You can add the leaves, stems or petals to a salad. They prefer a poor soil in full sun or part shade but are not fussy plants. Their height is around 50cm and spread 30cm.

Garlic cress (*Peltaria alliacea*)

The leaves often have a beautiful purple hue and make a very attractive addition to the salad garden. The main harvest season is autumn and early spring as the leaves can become bitter in the summer. They produce a mass of tiny white flowers in late spring which smell of honey. When flowering, the height is 60cm and spread 50cm.

Grecian bellflower (*Campanula versicolor*)

This is one of the nicest tasting perennial salad leaves and they are usually available all year. The leaves are quite small but the flowering stems will reach a height of anywhere between 30cm and 90cm.

Sorrel (*Rumex acetosa*)

The leaves are best harvested in spring and autumn and have a very strong zesty flavour. It will grow well in full sun or part shade and likes a moist, slightly acidic soil but isn't too fussy. It has a height and spread of 30-60cm.

Orpine (*Hylotelephium telephium*)

This is not my favourite salad leaf as it can be quite mucilaginous but some people love it. It is fleshy and crunchy so can add a different texture to a leafy salad. It needs full sun or it will get very tall and thin then flop over. They produce tight mounded heads of star-shaped flowers in late summer and into autumn which are loved by pollinators. They grow to around 50-75cm in height with a spread of 30-50cm.

Here sedum and oca are growing together in the garden at Earthed Up! in Belper. Both have edible leaves.

Allium 'Cameleon' is delicious, loved by bees and has a lovely quality of changing colour as the season progresses, starting pink and turning white before the blooms fade

Caucasian spinach (*Hablitzia tamnoides*)

This climber is great for smaller spaces because it can be trained upwards, it also loves semi-shade. It has a mild flavour similar to spinach. The young shoots can be eaten in spring or the leaves can be eaten through the summer months but may get tougher in the later months. They can grow up to 3m in length but can be cut back to keep to size.

Sweet cicely (*Myrrhis odorata*)

The leaves are downy-soft and can be used raw in salads to add some sweetness to otherwise predominantly bitter leaves. The leaves have an aromatic aniseed flavour that also work well in fruit salads to balance the acidity of some fruits. The leaves are available early in the year but their flavour is reduced when the plant is flowering. It grows to a height and spread of 1m.

Chives, garlic chives, Welsh onion, *Allium moly* (*Allium* sp.)

These are members of the onion family with tasty leaves that are tender enough to add to salads. Chives can be cut many times in a year as they keep springing back. Garlic chives have more garlicky leaves and the flowers are sweet. The Welsh onion's hollow stems are sliced thinly, similar to a spring onion. *Allium moly* is probably my favourite edible flower but the leaves are also tender, tasty and available early in the year.

Pink purslane (*Claytonia sibirica*)

This is a valuable plant as it is easy to grow; it will even grow in deep shade. It is not too fussy about soil type and has a mild flavour so can be used in quantity although it can get bitter in a hot summer if growing in dry soil. It grows to a height of just 20cm and will grow in poor soil, even acidic sandy soils.

Garlic mustard (*Alliaria petiolata*)

This plant is a biennial, meaning it makes leafy growth in its first year, then flowers and dies in its second year. I have added it here because it tends to self-seed profusely so once you have planted it, you tend to have it every year. It has very tasty garlic-flavoured leaves and reaches a height of 0.5-1m.

Bronze fennel grows happily with oregano in the herbaceous layer in a sunny spot

A hedge of saltbush at York Museum in their edible woodland garden

Fennel (*Foeniculum vulgare*)

This leaf has a strong aniseed flavour; not my favourite, but it does add a different flavour to salads that some people love. The leaves are very feathery and fine and you don't need many to get the fennel flavour. It prefers a moist but well-drained, fertile soil and needs full sun to thrive. It grows to a height of 1m.

Dandelion (*Taraxacum officinale*)

You probably have plenty of these in your garden already. The flavour is very bitter and many people force them to reduce this. As with forcing rhubarb, place an upturned pot, with a hole in the base, over the leaves for two to three weeks, then harvest the leaves straight away. This process makes the leaves much sweeter.

Apple mint (*Mentha suaveolens*)

Most mints are quite an overpowering flavour for salads, although this is sometimes desirable, but the soft furry leaves of apple mint are much milder. As with other mints, this can become invasive so contain it with a barrier. It prefers moist, fertile soil in sun or shade and grows to a height of around 50-75cm.

Scorzonera (*Pseudopodospermum hispanicum*)

Usually grown for its roots, the young tender shoots, leaves and petals can be added to salads. It has yellow flowers from June to September that look similar to a dandelion. It is not fussy about soil or light levels but it won't grow in full shade.

Saltbush (*Atriplex halimus*)

This is a shrubby plant with leaves that do indeed have a salty taste. Their distinctive taste is a great addition to salads. The leaves are small and silvery; it is an attractive evergreen shrub, meaning leaves are usually available year round. It can grow to a height of 2m. I have seen it grown as a very effective and dense hedge.

The young leaves of birch can be eaten but have a bitter taste

The hawthorn leaves are out quite early and are such a treat when you have gone without much leaf variety all winter

These lime leaves are too mature to eat now but these suckers make leaves much more accessible on a large tree

Edible tree leaves

These can be grown as a hedge, keeping the leaves at a harvestable height. Trimming the hedge can encourage a new flush of tender leaves. Tree leaves are very nutritious and could be a brilliant solution for future nature friendly, low maintenance, perennial food production.

Beech (*Fagus sylvatica*)

These leaves are only edible when young and just emerged but this can happen during two periods through the year, in spring then again in summer. They quickly become too tough to eat once mature. The flavour is quite mild so they can be used in bulk in a salad.

Birch (*Betula pendula*)

This is a very pretty tree and less easy to keep as a hedge than the other trees but it can be done as they respond well to pruning. The leaves are edible but have a hint of bitterness so are best used sparingly in salads.

Hawthorn (*Crataegus monogyna*)

I often have a nibble of hawthorn leaves from hedges while out walking in March and early April. The leaves are tasty and nutty when just emerging in spring and can be used in quantity. They have a folk name of 'bread and cheese' and are delicious when added to sandwiches.

Lime (*Tilia cordata*)

The flavour of these leaves is quite mild but some find them too mucilaginous and prefer to eat them in a sandwich where this is less noticeable. On large trees, you can often harvest the fresh young leaves over a long season from the base of the trunk where the suckers have been pruned. I am growing a small leaved lime (*Tilia cordata*) as a coppiced shrub so I can fit it into my small garden.

Red mulberry (*Morus rubra*)

Young red mulberry leaves have the best flavour but even with this species, the flavour can vary from mildly sweet to unpalatable so it is worth trying different trees then taking cuttings from any that you like. The leaves can cause a reaction in some people so, as with any new food, try a small quantity first.

Edible flowers

Edible flowers are a wonderful and colourful way to add diversity to your salads whilst also enhancing the beauty of your garden. Some can add a real punch of flavour too, especially herb flowers such as thyme, basil and sage. Daylily (*Hemerocallis* sp.) are delicious and I eat them as a snack while out in the garden. The whole flower bud can be used in a stir-fry but I like to wait until they open and add the individual petals. Nasturtium flowers have a lovely warm, spicy flavour and I find I can add quite a few of these to a salad. The leaves are also a great spicy salad leaf. Siberian bellflowers have a sweet, delicate flavour that can be easily overpowered by stronger tasting leaves so I find they are best used as a garnish rather than mixed in with other leaves. Turkish rocket is another plant that has taken a while to enjoy. The leaves tend to be cooked like spinach although they are more bitter. The flowers, on the other hand, smell like honey and I use them a lot in salads when they are in bloom and now grow Turkish rocket primarily as an edible flower crop.

Make sure when eating flowers that they have not been sprayed with anything. I would not recommend purchasing a flowering plant from a garden centre and eating the flowers straight away as you don't know what the plant has been fed with. It's good practice to either grow your own from seed or grow a newly acquired plant for a few months until hopefully any traces of plant feed in the compost has been washed out.

A mix of edible flowers and herbs can be used to sprinkle on soup or a pizza. Here I have a mix of chive flowers, kale flowers and oregano.

- *Allium moly*
- Bergamot (*Monarda didyma*)
- Borage (*Borago officinalis*)
- Carnation (*Dianthus caryophyllus*)
- All campanulas (*Campanula* sp.)
- Chamomile (*Chamaemelum nobile*)
- Chives *(Allium schoenoprasum)*
- *Chrysanthemum* sp.
- Clover (*Trifolium repens, T. pratense*)
- Cornflower (*Centaurea cyanus*)
- *Dahlia* sp.
- Daisy (*Bellis perennis*)
- Dandelion (*Taraxacum officinale*)
- Daylily (*Hemerocallis* sp.)
- Elderflower (*Sambucus nigra*)
- French marigold (*Tagetes patula*)
- Honeysuckle (*Lonicera periclymenum, L. japonica*)
- *Hosta* sp.
- Lavender (*Lavandula angustifolia, L. x intermedia*)
- Nasturtium (*Tropaeolum majus*)
- Pot marigold (*Calendula officinalis*)
- Primrose (*Primula vulgaris*)
- Rose (*Rosa* sp.)
- Rosemary (*Salvia rosmarinus*)
- Scented geranium (*Pelargonium* sp.)
- Sunflower (*Helianthus annuus*)
- Tulip (*Tulipa* sp.)
- Violets *(Viola tricolor, Viola sororia)*

Shade Garden

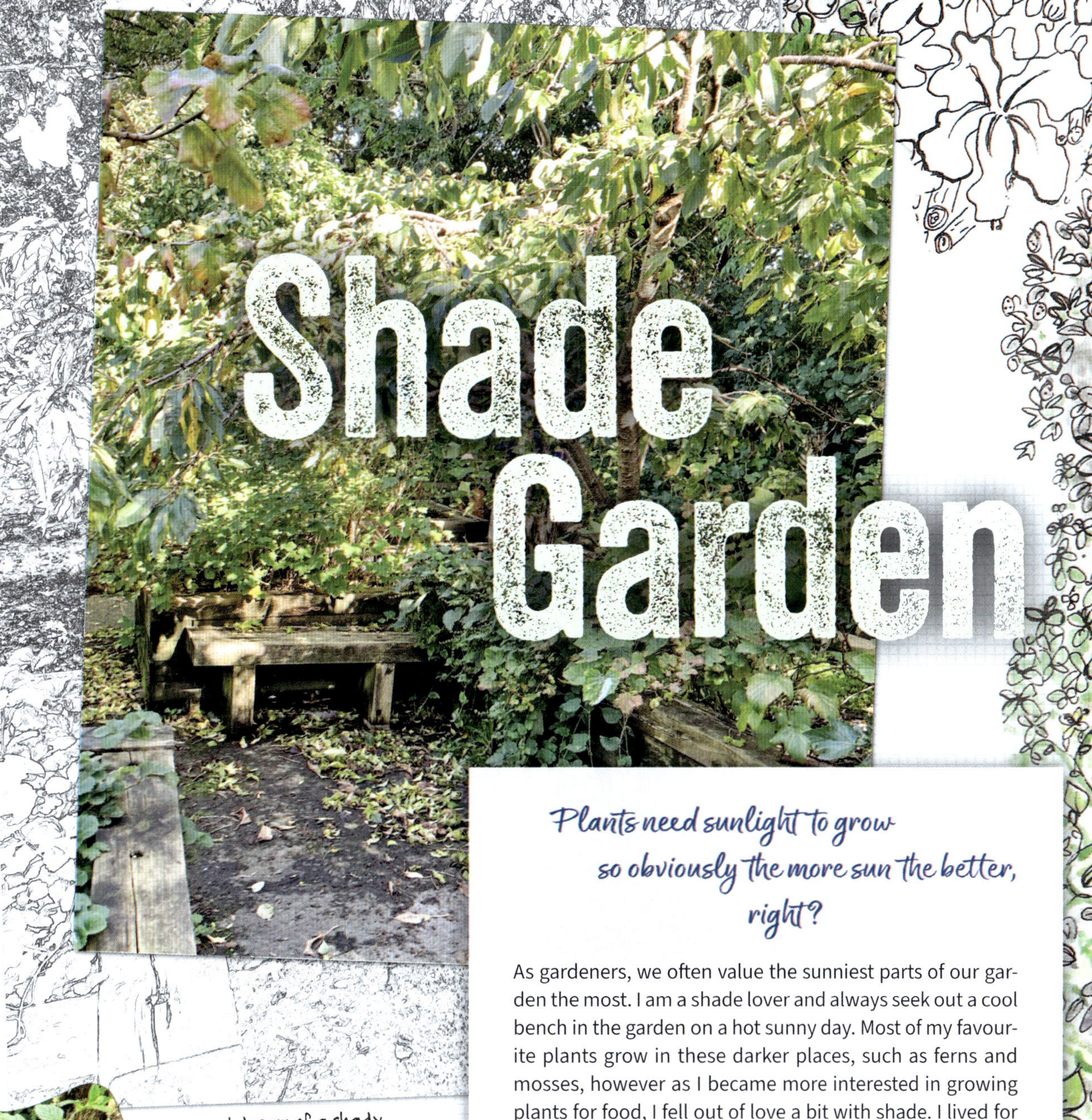

I dream of a shady bench like this one in the community forest garden in Lancaster. The whole garden is in raised beds sat on tarmac but is so lush and full of thriving plants.

Plants need sunlight to grow so obviously the more sun the better, right?

As gardeners, we often value the sunniest parts of our garden the most. I am a shade lover and always seek out a cool bench in the garden on a hot sunny day. Most of my favourite plants grow in these darker places, such as ferns and mosses, however as I became more interested in growing plants for food, I fell out of love a bit with shade. I lived for 15 years on a north facing slope that didn't see direct sunlight for six months of the year and this really restricted the selection of edible plants that would thrive in my garden. Having moved to a very sunny and exposed garden, I now realise how much I miss the cool, damp mossy corners of my previous garden and long for the trees to grow tall and their foliage to become dense enough to provide me with a shady spot to sit.

Design for a shady edible garden

I have designed this border to illustrate the large selection of plants that will grow with little direct sunlight. Some will thrive and some will grow but with less vigour than in a sunnier position. Deep shade usually means no direct sunlight at all, such as the north side of a building or under a tree. Part shade describes areas that receive some sun, around 3-6 hours a day, with full sun describing areas receiving direct sunlight for over six hours a day. But all shade is not equal. Some plants will make the most of the light limitations under a deciduous tree by getting going early in the year, putting up their shoots, leaves and flowers before the tree has put out its own leaves. Once the tree canopy gets too dense in summer, the plant dies down and becomes dormant until the following spring. These same plants will not necessarily do well under an evergreen tree which keeps its leaves, and therefore shade, year round. This is why shade gardens usually have more colour in spring and focus on foliage displays for the summer and autumn.

I have added some stone piles, or cairns, for wildlife habitat and to provide a surface for moss to grow on.

Cornus kousa var. *chinensis* is a woodland plant that thrives in semi-shade and produces edible fruits. It is a very ornamental shrub or small tree.

Mushroom logs leaning against a tree in the forest garden at the Centre for Alternative Technology in Wales

Shade in forest gardens

Forest gardens provide plenty of shady areas for edible plants, a few plants even thrive in very deep shade. However the aim is not to create shade. In fact the most common mistake made when designing a forest garden is planting trees too close together which limits the light reaching the lower canopies, causing the lower layers to be unproductive or die out all together. The best way to remedy this is to remove some of the trees. If you are currently designing a forest garden, make sure you have taken into account the eventual canopy size of your trees and large shrubs and leave plenty of room around each one for light to reach the lower layers.

Removing the lower branches of trees and shrubs, known as crown lifting, allows more light to their base and planting to be extended right underneath. This is a very effective way of using the vertical space and maximising the yield from your garden. This technique can be used on fruit and ornamental trees but also on shrubs such as currants, jostaberry, gooseberry, mahonia and bamboo. I have also crown lifted a huge perennial kale 'Taunton Deane' by staking its main stem and training it into a tree. It is usually a sprawling shrub but by adding a support, I could lift the branches off the ground and plant rosemary, sage, chives, geraniums and iris underneath.

Growing mushrooms on logs

Mushrooms are one crop that requires shade although I have struggled to get a decent crop of mushrooms from logs despite trying several times. You can buy either wooden plugs, straw or sawdust inoculated with your chosen mushroom. You can even get spore syringes but these mean a single use plastic syringe goes to landfill. These are not detailed 'how to' instructions here; I want to give you an idea of what is involved so you can decide if you have the right conditions and might like to try mushroom growing.

The easiest mushrooms to grow on logs are shitake and oyster mushrooms. Each mushroom likes specific types of wood and the wood is actually their food source, not just something for them to grow on. Shitake grows well on oak or maple logs; oyster mushrooms prefer white birch but will grow on oak, maple or willow. Fungi are not plants so do not require sunlight for photosynthesis but they do still need water and a food source. I think the reason my mushroom logs failed to fruit may be because I did not know to water my logs regularly in dry weather. If the fungi dries out, it will die. So ensure you have a source of water nearby and water once or twice a week in hot, dry weather.

Your log must be freshly cut from a healthy tree. This is to ensure the wood is not already contaminated with another fungi which may produce mushrooms that are not edible. Once cut, leave your log to dry out for up to a month to allow the wood to die, allowing the tree's natural fungicides to be released and used up, otherwise this kills the spores you are adding. Fungi will not be able to colonise wood that is still alive. Following instructions from your kit, drill holes and hammer in your plugs, or insert your inoculated material. Cover the holes with melted wax (not beeswax) to keep moisture in and contaminants out then lean your log against a wall or fence somewhere shady and damp. Keeping the log off the floor prevents contamination from the ground. You can stack the logs in a tower, a bit like stacking jenga blocks, if you have many logs and not much space. You should get your first harvest in 6-12 months and hopefully your log should produce flushes of mushrooms for several years.

Plants for shade

Most of these plants have been mentioned in previous designs so I will refer you to the relevant page where that is the case.

Trees

Cherry 'Morello' (*Prunus cerasus*)

This cherry has very acidic fruits which are best for making jams, jellies and pies where you can add sugar. The dark red fruits ripen in July and August. They are small bushy trees up to a maximum of 4m tall and are self-fertile. They are very tolerant of shade and can be grown against a north-facing wall.

Plum 'Czar' (*Prunus domestica*)

Whilst this plum will not fruit well in a lot of shade, it is more shade tolerant than most plums. It is a compact tree and grows to 2.5-4m depending on rootstock. It has pretty white blossoms in spring and deep blue fruit which ripen in early August.

Pear 'Beth' (*Pyrus communis*)

Pears do need some sun but 'Beth' will fruit well with just a few hours of sunlight a day. The fruit is small but sweet and ripens in September. It needs a pollinator (group 3) so if no neighbours have a tree flowering at the same time you can either plant a different pear in a sunny location or find a flowering sprig from a pear you have access to and place it in a jar of water near the tree so pollinators visit the sprig and pollinate your tree.

Chinese pepper tree (*Zanthoxylum simulans*)

This pepper tree can grow in full shade. It's a small tree or shrub growing up to 4m. The leaves are edible and have a spicy, citrus smell and an unusual flavour. It is mainly grown for its pink peppercorns which appear in autumn and can be used like pepper in a grinder. The bright pink/red fruits split open to reveal shiny hard black seeds. It is the peppercorn case that has most of the flavour but the seeds can also be ground. It is an ingredient of Chinese five spice and it has a numbing, cooling effect on the tongue so use sparingly. It prefers a well-drained, fertile soil.

Shrubs

Raspberries 'Malling Jewel' and 'Octavia' (*Rubus idaeus*)

See jam guild, p.50, for details.

Gooseberry (*Ribes uva-crispa*)

See jam guild, p.50, for details.

Jostaberry (*Ribes* x *nidigrolaria*)

This is a cross between a blackcurrant and a gooseberry. It is quite sweet so it can be eaten as a dessert berry. It can grow much bigger than either a blackcurrant or a gooseberry and I have found them to be very resistant to pest and disease attacks.

Red, white and pink currants (*Ribes rubrum*)

All these cultivars of *Ribes rubrum* are much more shade tolerant than blackcurrants. You can find sweet

It is mainly the outer pink seed casing of the Chinese pepper tree that has the pepper flavour and aroma but you can eat the whole seed too

Raspberries growing with solomon seal, wild garlic and creeping comfrey varieties for eating as dessert fruit but I tend to grow them for making jellies, such as redcurrant jelly. They can be grown as a bush growing to a height and spread of 1.5m or trained against a wall or fence where space is limited. The fruits ripen around April or May.

Mahonia aquifolium has holly-like leaves and these fragrant yellow flowers in spring

Mahonia 'Charity' is a beautiful evergreen shrub and one of my favorite scents in the winter garden

Blackcurrants (*Ribes nigrum*)

These are less tolerant of shade than *Ribes rubrum* but I have had good harvests from a blackcurrant in almost full shade, growing under a tree. The fruit will be sweeter in a sunnier spot but you will still get fruit in shady gardens.

Oregon grape (*Mahonia aquifolium*)

This shrub produces large clusters of strongly scented flowers in spring, followed by edible dark blue berries. Evergreen holly-like leaves can make picking the fruits quite painful without the use of gloves. It grows to a height of 1m and a spread of 1-1.5m and prefers shade, growing happily in full shade.

Oregon grape 'Charity' (*Mahonia* x *media)*

See food forest border, p.43, for more details.

Chinese dogwood (*Cornus kousa*)

This cornus will grow in full sun but it will grow happily in part shade. It is fairly untroubled by pests and diseases, tolerates a wide range of soils and is an absolutely beautiful small tree. In summer it is covered with white bracts with a tiny white flower in the centre and has vivid bronze and red autumn colours in autumn. The pink/red fruits are edible and taste a bit like mango but they can have a grainy, gritty texture; the flavour is lovely so I don't mind too much. The maximum height is 7m but it can be pruned to keep it smaller.

Elder 'Black Lace' (*Sambucus nigra*)

This elder has beautiful dark purple lacy leaves that look almost black. Elder will grow well in even deep shade but the fruit is sweeter if they have a bit of sun. It produces flat umbels of pale pink flowers in late spring, followed by dark purple/black berries. It grows up to 3m but responds well to coppicing if you want to keep it smaller. I like to make champagne from the flowers.

Golden bamboo (*Phyllostachys aurea*)

I have grown this successfully in quite a lot of shade. It is an evergreen bamboo with canes up to 3.5m in height. The older canes are a golden colour and very useful for making supports in the garden. You can also eat the new shoots as they emerge from the ground in spring. There is often hesitation about planting bamboo but I grew this one for 15 years and it didn't spread far. If you are concerned, you can add a barrier when planting.

Herbaceous

Hosta sp.

See tropical style food forest garden, p.73, for more details.

Sweet cicely (*Myrrhis odorata*)

See perennial salad garden, p.XX, for more details.

Good King Henry (*Blitum bonus-henricus*)

See food forest border, p.57, for more details.

Lemon balm (*Melissa officinalis*)

See mini forest garden, p.34, for more details.

Garlic mustard (*Alliaria petiolata*)

See perennial salad garden, p.57, for more details.

Giant bellflower (*Campanula latifolia*)

This campanula grows up to 1.5m tall with large edible purple/blue flowers in summer. You can also eat the young shoots raw or cooked. It will grow happily in part shade.

Solomon seal (*Polygonatum multiflorum*)

The young shoots are eaten like asparagus and have a good flavour with only a hint of bitterness. They will thrive in deep shade and are pretty drought tolerant. The plants can be defoliated by the solomon seal sawfly larvae in early summer but they usually bounce back. They grow up to 1.2m in height and 30-50cm in spread.

Big root cranesbill (*Geranium macrorrhizum*)

This plant forms a very effective ground cover with dense foliage. It will grow in deep shade, is drought tolerant

Chinese dogwood fruit looks exotic and tastes a bit like mango

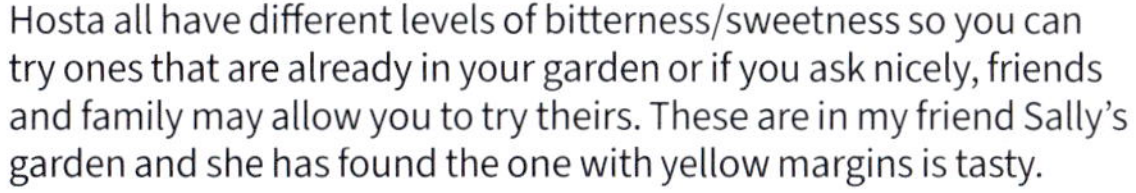

Hosta all have different levels of bitterness/sweetness so you can try ones that are already in your garden or if you ask nicely, friends and family may allow you to try theirs. These are in my friend Sally's garden and she has found the one with yellow margins is tasty.

I have grown Good King Henry in a few different shady spots and it seems to thrive in both slightly damp and quite dry shade

and has lovely autumn colours. Its leaves can be used in potpourri or for perfume and its flowers are good for pollinators. It grows to a maximum height of 50cm but its spread can be indefinite if left to its own devices.

Star-flowered lily of the valley (*Smilacina stellata*)

This is a woodland plant and is very happy in the shade of trees. It is a creeping, rhizomatous perennial with stems growing to 60cm tall and wide. It flowers in late summer then produces bitter sweet edible berries in autumn. The young leaves are also edible raw or cooked and the young shoots can be eaten like asparagus. It likes a fairly neutral, moist but well-drained soil.

Udo (*Aralia cordata*)

This vegetable is huge, growing from ground level to 2m in height by mid summer. The young shoots are eaten in spring but can be quite fiddly to prepare. They are a very attractive plant that will grow happily in deep shade where choices are limited so it is still worth growing.

Pachyphragma macrophylla grows well as a ground cover in shade. It is one of the first plants to flower in the year.

Ground cover

Iceland moss (*Sedum ternatum*)

This ground hugging, evergreen succulent grows to 15cm in height. Its fleshy leaves can be eaten in salads in small amounts. In summer it has small white starry flowers. It is a rockery plant and likes well-drained soils.

Pink purslane (*Claytonia sibirica*)

See perennial salad garden design, p.57, for more details.

Bugle (*Ajuga reptans*)

See tropical style food forest design, p.73, for more details.

Wood sorrel (*Oxalis acetosella*)

This is a tiny plant at just 8cm tall. It has strong lemony-flavoured leaves which are high in oxalic acid so only eat small amounts. It is a woodland-floor plant so will grow even in deep shade.

Lungwort (*Pulmonaria officinalis*)

One of my favourite spring-flowering plants, lungwort thrives in deep shade. The leaves taste bland and can be a bit hairy but are okay in salads in small quantities; their main use is as an apothecary plant. It is evergreen, so leaves are available year round and its flowers are loved by pollinators, especially bees, in spring.

Pachyphragma macrophylla

The leaves are edible but not very tasty. I grow it mainly as a pollinator plant and for ground cover. It has white flowers in spring. It grows in most soils, including heavy clay soil, and prefers deep or part shade. It is a low growing plant at 30cm in height.

Landcress (*Barbarea verna*)

This is a biennial but it happily self-seeds in the right conditions. It has hot, spicy small leaves, similar to watercress, and can be picked over a long season.

Almost too pretty to eat, the Erythroniums look beautiful in a spring woodland

Honeysuckle has long been one of my favourite plants in the garden. I have learnt to collect its flowers to use in herbal tea.

It is quite small at 30cm tall. It prefers a cool, moist and fertile soil and will tolerate deep shade.

Root

Dog's tooth violet
(*Erythronium dens-canis, E. revolutum* 'Pagoda')

These are small spring-flowering bulbs growing to a height of 15-30cm. The bulbs are edible and ready for harvesting from early summer until early winter. They can be eaten raw or cooked and are sometimes ground into flour. They are, however, very pretty, almost too pretty to dig up and eat.

Climbers

Caucasian spinach (*Hablitzia tamnoides*)

See perennial salad garden, p.57, for more details.

Honeysuckle (*Lonicera periclymenum*)

This vigorous, twining climber can grow up to 6m in length. You can suck the base of flowers to extract the nectar or add the flowers to salad. Honeysuckle is an important food for many caterpillars including the rare white admiral. It is a woodland plant so will grow well in the shade.

Chocolate vine (*Akebia quinata*)

This is a vigorous climber growing up to 12m long. It flowers in spring and produces fruit in late summer which is edible but not hugely tasty. The soft young shoots can be eaten in salads or pickled. It is both shade and drought tolerant so great for those tricky spots in the garden where not much else will grow.

Plant list for the shade garden design

Big root cranesbill (*Geranium macrorrhizum*)
Siberian bugloss 'Jack Frost' (*Brunnera macrophylla*)
Bugle (*Ajuga reptans*)
Caucasian spinach (*Hablitzia tamnoides*)
Cherry 'Morello' (*Prunus cerasus*)
Chinese dogwood (*Cornus kousa*)
Chinese pepper tree (*Zanthoxylum simulans*)
Chocolate vine (*Akebia quinata*)
Giant bellflower (*Campanula latifolia*)
Gooseberry 'Hinnonmaki Green' (*Ribes uva-crispa*)
Jostaberry (*Ribes* x *nidigrolaria*)
Lady's mantle (*Alchemilla mollis*)
Masterwort 'White Giant' (*Astrantia major*)
Oregon grape (*Mahonia aquifolium*)
Pachyphragma macrophylla
Pink currant (*Ribes rubrum*)
Rhubarb 'Stockbridge Arrow' (*Rheum* x *hybridum)*
Solomon seal (*Polygonatum multiflorum*)
Star-flowered lily of the valley (*Smilacina stellata*)
Sweet cicely (*Myrrhis odorata*)
Udo (*Aralia cordata*)

Planting plan for the shady edible garden

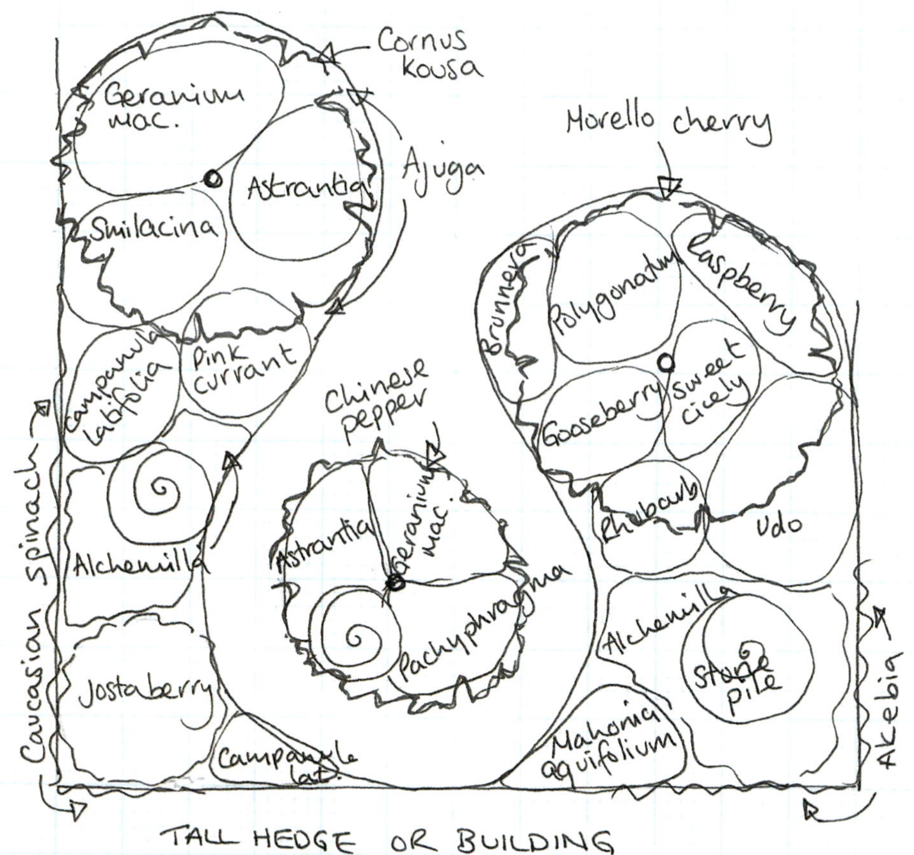

Tropical Style Food Forest

The brainstorming collage for the tropical style food forest

I love to set myself challenges with my planting designs.

Creating a garden full of edible and useful plants should not hold you back from being ambitious with how it will look and the atmosphere you can create. I was challenged by a client to produce a design that looked subtropical and I fully embraced the task. Subtropical plants often have large leaves and bright coloured flowers so these are the extra parameters I set myself. I wanted the plants to be fully hardy as much as possible (although I did break this rule a bit) because a food forest is all about creating a resilient ecosystem, and having to replant each year is certainly not resilient. Self-seeders are fine as they will look after themselves and find places to germinate and grow.

A plan view of the tropical style food forest

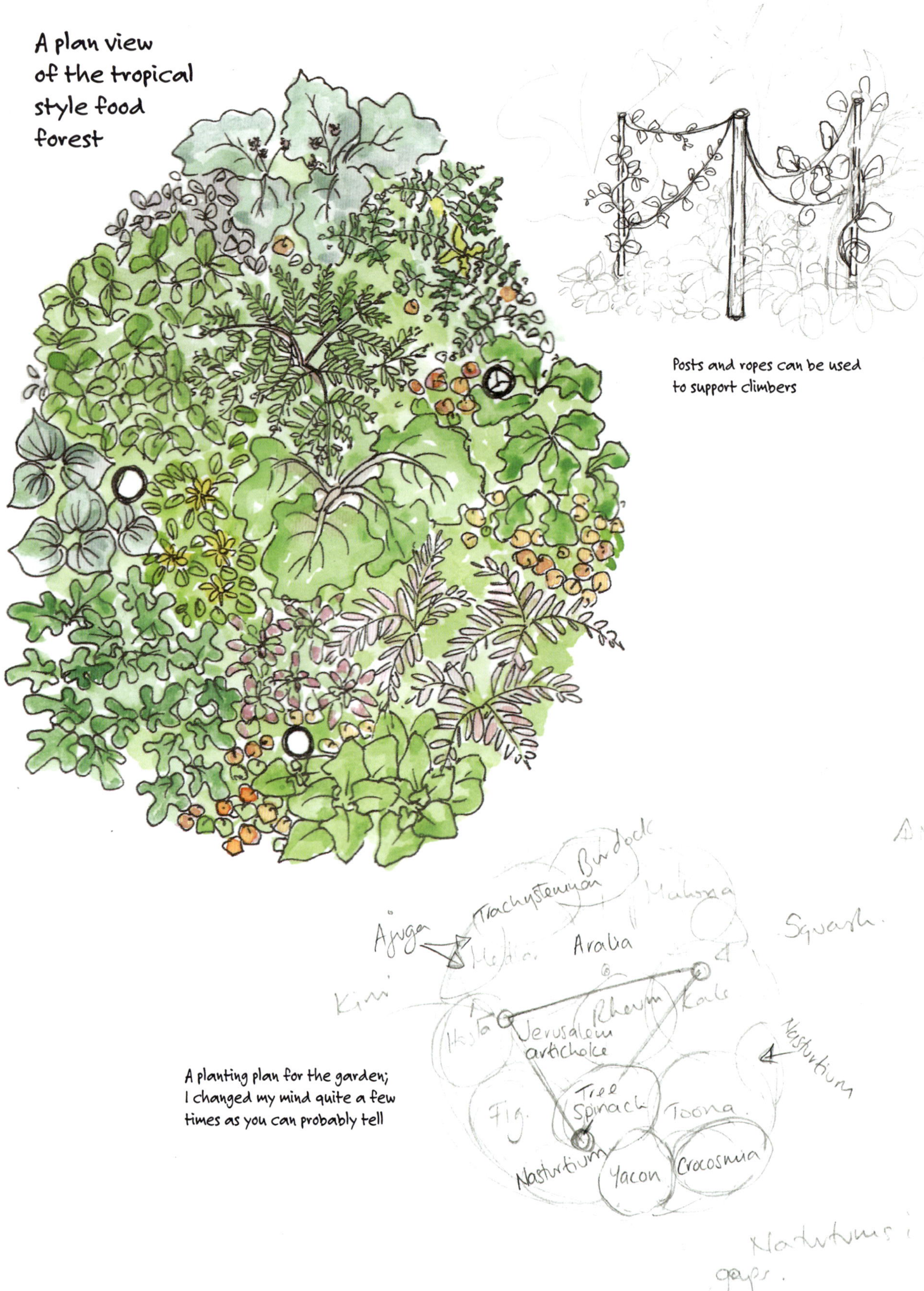

Posts and ropes can be used to support climbers

A planting plan for the garden; I changed my mind quite a few times as you can probably tell

It was fun to reassess plants according to their leaf shape and to design something totally different to the usual gardens I design. It made me look at plants like rhubarb in a different way; celebrating its large leaves rather than just the stems, and growing hardy bananas for their useful leaves rather than being disappointed that you won't get a crop of fruit. New Zealand flax can often look out of place in a garden full of flowers but its striking sculptural sword-like leaves can really sing in a tropical style setting. There is still room for plenty of pollinator plants but choosing ones with bright colours such as crocosmia 'Lucifer' and nasturtium 'Empress of India' and dahlia 'Bishop of Llandaff' helps give the impression of a hot and humid climate.

Medlar are a weird and wonderful looking fruit with large leaves, perfect for that exotic look

Plant list

Trees

Chinese cedar (*Toona sinensis*)

The young leaves and shoots of *Toona* are edible and have a savoury flavour which led to the nickname of 'beef and onions'. The tree can grow up to 15m if left unpruned but they respond well to coppicing to keep them small. If coppicing, you will likely cut off any flowers but they have long white pendant panicles up to 70cm long in summer. If coppiced you should be able to keep it to a height and spread of around 2-3m. *Toona* prefers full sun and a fertile, well-drained but moist soil but is otherwise fairly unfussy about soil type. The variegated version 'Flamingo' is bright pink and is said to be just as tasty if not more so.

Medlar 'Nottingham' (*Mespilus germanica*)

This small tree has beautiful large leathery leaves, perfect for the subtropical look, with the benefit of good autumn colour. They produce white flowers in the spring followed by delicious fruit in the autumn which need to be left to 'blet' before eating. Ideally they like full sun although I have one happily growing in quite a lot of shade. They will also tolerate a wide range of soil types. The eventual size they could reach is a height and spread of 4-8m.

Angelica tree (*Aralia elata*)

The young shoots of this attractive small tree can be cooked and eaten; they are popular in Korea and Japan. The tree also has medicinal properties. It has very unusual-looking spiny stems, divided leaves up to 1m in length and produces a mass of creamy white flowers on panicles in late summer to autumn. It prefers full sun and a well-drained, moist soil and can tolerate poor soils. It can reach a height of 7m and a spread of 6m or even bigger on fertile soils. It can spread by suckers but does it slowly and so is easy to keep under control.

The leaves of *Aralia* look very jungle-like. The flowers are pretty spectacular too.

Shrubs

Fig 'Brunswick' (*Ficus carica*)

Figs fruit best when planted against a wall or in a sunny sheltered place. Their large lobed leaves look very jungly. (See mini forest garden, p.34, for more details.)

Oregon grape 'Charity' (*Mahonia x media*)

This striking shrub, with divided leaves up to 30cm long, has delicious edible fruit in summer. You have to cook them before eating them; the flavour is similar to blackcurrant without the tartness. The yellow flowers in winter are a great source of pollen and nectar and are so fragrant you often smell a mahonia before you see it. They are a woodland plant and prefer a slightly acidic, moist but well-drained soil. They also prefer shade and need protection from full sun and strong winds. They can reach a height of up to 4m but can be pruned to be quite upright and underplanted. The spread of a full grown shrub is around 2-3m.

Perennial kale 'Taunton Deane' (*Brassica oleracea* Acephala group)

This is my favourite perennial kale with its huge blue/green leaves with purple midribs. It grows up to 2m tall although I have staked it as a tree and it reached almost 3m. It tends to be a sprawling shrub, up to 2m across, but regular harvesting can keep it small. It can be short-lived but is very easy to grow on cuttings: simply push a cutting in the ground or in a pot as a replacement. The leaves look tough but are delicious when lightly steamed and are available year round as it is evergreen. It rarely flowers but when it does, the flowers are edible in salads. I have found it is happy in most soils but doesn't like to dry out or get too wet.

The leaves of kale 'Taunton Deane' can be huge if they are in fertile soil but still tender and delicious to eat. I love then lightly steamed.

Herbaceous

Hosta 'Big Daddy' (*Hosta sieboldiana*)

This herbaceous perennial has impressive, large chalky blue/green leaves. Hosta can be plagued by slugs but this one has tough leaves and is less prone to damage. The new shoots in spring can be eaten in a stir-fry or salad and the flowers are also edible. 'Empress Wu' is another large and tasty hosta growing to a height of 90-120cm with a spread of 1-1.8m. Hostas like moist soil and tolerate waterlogged soils. They will grow in full sun to full shade but will grow larger in sunnier spots so long as the soil is moist. The purple flowers appear in June/July.

Montbretia 'Lucifer' (*Crocosmia* sp.)

This plant is rich in pollen and nectar so is a great choice to attract pollinators. The large red exotic looking flowers appear in the summer above the strap like leaves. 'Lucifer' is a large cultivar that can grow to a height of 1.5-2m with a spread of 50cm. Its tall upright habit means it can be underplanted. It is not too fussy about soil type but it doesn't like waterlogged soil and is happiest in full sun.

Tree spinach (*Chenopodium giganteum*)

This plant can grow huge despite being an annual. It self-seeds so once you have it, you shouldn't need to sow it again but you may want to transplant seedlings to a position of your choice. The leaves are used as a spinach substitute and are ideally cooked to reduce the level of saponins. The young leaves are a striking magenta pink with a coating that looks like they are covered in glitter. It is a tall plant and can grow up to 2.4m although not very wide at around 0.5-1m. It prefers a sunny spot but can tolerate some shade.

Burdock (*Arctium lappa*)

The roasted roots of burdock taste a bit like a cross between sweet chestnut and parsnip and are harvested in autumn. Leaves can be used to wrap foods for cooking or to transport. The roots and leaves also have medicinal properties. Plants are biennial and best harvested after the first year's growth before flowering. They grow to a height of 1-2m with a similar spread. The leaves are large so give it plenty of room. Flower spikes with thistle-like 'sticky buds' appear in late summer in the second year and are a great pollinator plant, especially for butterflies.

There are several sizes and colours of *Crocosmia* available, I like the fiery colours of this 'Lucifer' with red *Helenium*

The sticky buds of burdock are a childhood favourite to throw at people's clothing

Early-flowering borage
(*Trachystemon orientalis*)

The flowers, shoots and stems of this plant are edible and eaten in Turkey as a wild food. The plant is covered in rough hairs which look unappealing so I have never eaten this plant. I grow it because its small, borage-like flowers come out in late winter and are loved by pollinators and it grows well in dry shade where not many other plants will grow. With its huge leaves, it can grow to 50-60cm tall with a spread of around 1m although it can become invasive without competition.

The leaves of *Trachystemmon* are impressively large and tropical looking but it is very easy to grow and it loves deep shade

Rhubarb (*Rheum x hybridum*)

This is a well loved and traditional crop for the home garden but it can be a very ornamental plant. The stems are used to make desserts, jam and wine. The leaves of some varieties can be huge. Rhubarb 'Goliath' has a height and spread of 1m and delicious tender stems. Rhubarb likes full sun or part shade and a moist but well-drained soil. It tends to die down early in the year so is best positioned away from the front of a border so the ugly dying leaves can be hidden.

Chinese rhubarb (*Rheum palmatum*)

Related to rhubarb, this variety is eaten in the same way but is much more ornamental. Its leaves grow up to 75cm long and its flowers, blooming in June/July, can reach 2m in height. The plant has a spread of around 2m. It is also used medicinally in China. It is often planted in bog gardens and prefers a moist soil but is not fussy about the pH. It will grow in semi-shade or full sun.

Yarrow in the border at Ecology Building Society

Ground cover

Bugle 'Catlin's Giant' (*Ajuga reptans*)

It is evergreen, forming a mat of purple leaves which make a fabulous contrast to other plants in the garden. The purple/blue flowering spires, appearing in May, only grow to a maximum of 30cm but they are very popular with bees. The leaves are edible but not that tasty, their value is mainly as a pollinator plant. They can spread quite far if they are happy in a shady spot with moist soil. They can tolerate a wide range of soils in shade or sun but don't like to dry out too much. 'Catlins Giant' has larger leaves and is more vigorous than most *Ajuga* varieties so is perfect for a more exotic look.

Nasturtium 'Empress of India' (*Tropaeolum majus*)

There are many varieties of this self-seeding annual available in shades of yellow, orange, red or pink. This variety has vibrant orange flowers against a backdrop of blue/green leaves which makes the flowers appear to be glowing. 'Empress of India' will trail across the ground as a ground cover but also climbs up any available branches. All parts of the plant are edible. I use the flowers and leaves in salads and the seed pods can be used as a substitute for capers and are often pickled. They prefer well-drained but moist soil and full sun although they will tolerate some shade. The flowers usually appear from July onwards until the plants are killed by frost so you get a long season of harvest.

Roots

Jerusalem artichoke 'Fuseau' (*Helianthus tuberosus*)

A relative of the sunflower, these have a pretty yellow flower in summer. They are an old fashioned winter vegetable as you eat the root tubers once the plant has died back at the end of the year. Simply leave a few tubers in the ground after harvesting and you will have some each year. Jerusalem artichokes grow very tall at 1.8-2.4m, even the smaller variety 'Dwarf Sunray' grows to 1.5-1.8m but they can be used to create a lush backdrop to a border. They are pretty tough plants and prefer a moist, well-drained soil but can tolerate some drying out. They don't like waterlogged soil as the tubers will rot. The plants are tall and narrow so the spread of each plant is only 50-75cm.

Yacon 'Inca Red' (*Smallanthus sonchifolius*)

Yacon are not fully hardy in the UK so in colder areas you may need to pot up a few tubers and overwinter in a frost-free place in case those in the ground don't survive the winter. If leaving some tubers in the ground, give them a deep mulch to act as insulation. This effort is well worth it for the lush and tropical looking foliage of yacon. Plants grow to a height of 1.8m with a spread of 1m and certainly give that tropical feel of a food forest in a warmer climate. The tubers are harvested in the autumn, before the first frosts. They look like a potato but are often eaten like a fruit with a taste and texture a bit like a crunchy pear.

Ajuga 'Catlins Giant' has very large leaves and flower spikes compared to the other varieties. Its leaves look very lush when grown in the shade and are different shades of purple and green giving a fabulous contrast to orange and red flowers.

Nasturtiums come in many shades of yellow, pink, orange and red and are a very effective creeping annual that will fill gaps quickly underneath and between shrubs and trees

Squash creating a very jungly archway in a glasshouse at Hulme Community Garden Centre

Climbers

Summer squash 'Trombonchino' (*Cucurbita moschata*)

This annual variety is related to butternut squash but is eaten like a courgette. It grows on long trailing vines which can be trained up wires, fences or trellising. The large leaves look fabulous amongst other subtropical looking plants. We grow squash and other pumpkins up washing line ropes and out across our garden as they take up so much room on the ground. The squash are long and curved and can be eaten when small or left to grow to over 50cm and are still just as tender and tasty. The vines will grow to several meters in length and will need tying in regularly to prevent them snapping in windy positions. You can grow any pumpkin in this way and even quite large fruits can be trained upwards without the need for extra support for the fruit. As with all squash, they will thrive in a well-drained, moist and very fertile soil. If you have poor soil, I would recommend creating a planting pit and adding plenty of compost and liquid feeding weekly throughout the growing season to get good-sized vines.

Kiwi 'Jenny' (*Actinidia deliciosa*)

'Jenny' is the only hardy, self-fertile kiwi I know of so is my go to variety, particularly for colder areas. The fruit are much smaller than the kiwi you buy in the shops but nothing beats the satisfaction of growing one yourself. Kiwi 'Jenny' is also a very ornamental climber with large heart shaped leaves and clusters of pretty white flowers in early summer. It is a vigorous climber growing to 6m so could be trained up a wall, over a pergola or along a fence. I have also slung ropes between trees and trained climbers along those to give the feeling of being in a jungle. They tolerate a wide range of soils and soil moisture but prefer a moist and slightly acidic soil.

The trombonchino squash are prolific and produce many sweet and tender fruit through the summer

Other edible and useful plants for a tropical look

Agapanthus sp.

Bamboo (*Fargesia* sp.)

Phyllostachys sp.

Bergenia sp.

Canna sp.

Cardoon (*Cynara cardunculus*)

Dahlia sp.

Darmera peltata

Daylily (*Hemerocallis* sp.)

Fatsia japonica

Hops (*Humulus lupulus*)

Ligularia sp.

Osmunda regalis

Purple hazel 'Purpurea' (*Corylus maxima*)

Yucca sp.

Udo (*Aralia cordata*)

Pallet Planter

When you are growing in small gardens, you need to maximise your planting opportunities by using the vertical space. The yard at our previous house was mostly paved, with limited soil for planting. We also wanted to make the most of the lovely sunny south-facing wall, and pallet planters seemed the perfect solution.

This pansy is perennial and a beautiful blue colour that really stands out amongst green salad leaves

When building a pallet planter you can add plants to the top as well as the front and back

The children were quite young when we built our first planters and the height was perfect for them to forage, especially for the tiny jewel-like wild strawberries conveniently hanging below the foliage. Plants are less prone to slug attack as they are off the ground, and salad leaves are kept clean as there is no open soil to get splashed onto them. We mainly grow salad plants which would struggle to compete in our forest garden beds and include annual herbs such as parsley, basil and coriander. Flowers can be added for colour. My favourite are violas, especially the large-flowered pansies that can be added to salads or used to decorate cakes.

A single pallet can be lined with plastic, ideally reclaimed plastic such as old compost bags. This will prolong the life of the wood if the compost is not in direct contact with the pallet and keep the compost in place; keeping it moist for longer. Slits can be cut in the plastic liner in the spaces between the timbers in the front of the pallet and plants inserted into the compost. You can add a layer of hessian sacking before the plastic if you don't want to see the black plastic, although the foliage of the plants quickly covers any gaps. You can also plant into the top of the planter. This means you get a large planting area whilst only taking up a very small footprint in your garden.

We found that the compost dried out very quickly with a single pallet so we decided to attach two pallets together to get twice as much compost. This stays moist for longer, reducing the amount of time spent watering and reduces stress on the plants. Some pallets have wooden planks on both faces, if this is the case, remove the planks from one face of the pallets then join them together back to back. We chained the pallets to the wall to prevent them from falling over until Andrew's dad had the smart idea to splay out the base of the pallets to make more of a wedge shape which made them very stable and enabled us to place them around the yard even in places where there was no wall to attach to, creating free-standing planters which could have both sides planted up. We have tried out other green wall systems but I have yet to find one to beat the simplicity of the pallet planter.

When planting up your pallet, there is room in the top for tall upright plants. I planted a rosemary (*Salvia rosmarinus*) into the top as it provided perfect free-draining conditions for Mediterranean herbs. A variety such as 'Roman Beauty' only grows to 40cm in height. I planted thyme (*Thymus vulgaris*) either side of the rosemary as it never seemed to like the cold wet soil in my yard but thrived in the top of the planter. As a rule, plant the smaller things at the top and the larger plants at the bottom, this way the plants lower down shouldn't get shaded out.

This green wall at Ecology Building Society, Silsden, was made using purpose built plastic planters but is very high maintenance as each planting pocket is very small

You can be creative with what materials you use to create a wall planter. At High Adventure in Cowling, they used large catering tins to plant into.

Plants suitable for your pallet planter

Annuals

Basil (*Ocimum basilicum*)

Buck's horn plantain (*Plantago coronopus*) is a slightly tender perennial so it will survive in milder areas but may act as an annual in cold winters.

Dwarf nasturtium (*Tropaeolum majus*)

Garden pansy (*Viola* x *wittrockiana*)

Land cress (*Barbarea verna*)

Lettuce (*Lactuca sativa*)

Pak choi (*Brassica rapa* subsp. *chinensis*)

Parsley (*Petroselinum crispum*)

Pot marigold (*Calendula officinalis*)

Swiss chard (*Beta vulgaris* subsp. *vulgaris* Cicla group)

Winter purslane (*Claytonia perfoliata*)

Perennials

Alpine strawberry (*Fragaria vesca*)

Broadleaf plantain (*Plantago major*)

Garlic chives (*Allium tuberosum*)

Perennial wall rocket (*Diplotaxis tenuifolia*)

Ribwort plantain (*Plantago lanceolata*)

Salad burnet (*Sanguisorba minor*)

Siberian bellflower (*Campanula poscharskyana*)

Siberian purslane (*Claytonia sibirica*)

Sorrel (*Rumex acetosa*)

Strawberry (*Fragaria* x *ananassa*)

Thyme (*Thymus vulgaris*)

Trailing rosemary (*Salvia rosmarinus* Prostratus group)

Campanula poscharskyana grows well in a pallet planter and will grow in the shade. It provides edible salad leaves year round.

Thyme can grow well in a pallet planter. It prefers growing either in the top or along the top of the front so it doesn't get shaded out.

Nasturtium and alpine strawberry mingling well in a green wall

The first aid kit garden designed to mimic the cross on the top of a first aid box with paths to allow access to all the beds

Healing Gardens

Making use of nature's pharmacy

The last few years have been an exciting journey of discovery for me, uncovering the powerful healing properties of many plants that I have grown for years as ornamentals in my garden.

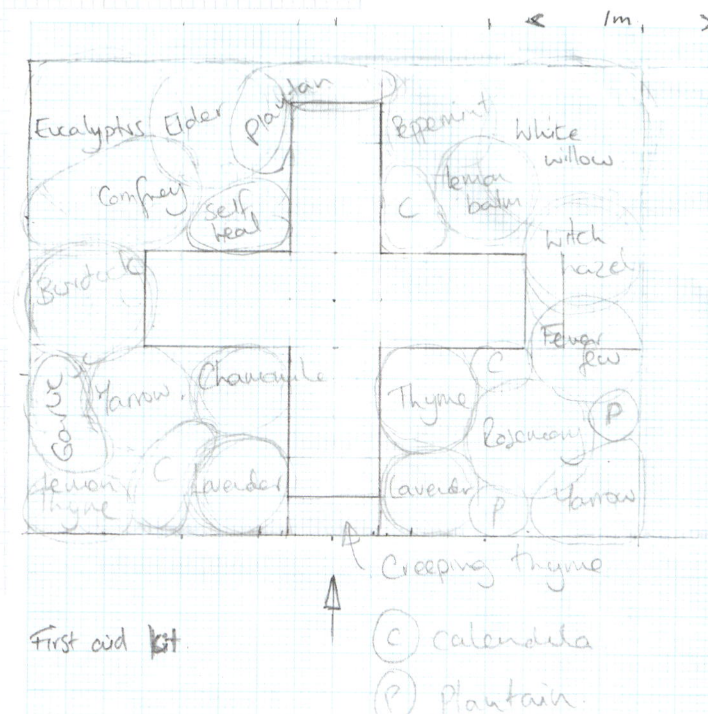

Planting plan for the first aid kit garden

Herbal first aid kit

Modern medicine has come up with some amazing pills and potions to help us to live longer and healthier lives. They have been so successful that the many herbal plants that have been used for hundreds if not thousands of years for minor ailments and first aid are now overlooked. Synthetic medicines often come with horrible side effects which can be worse than the ailment you were trying to cure. I have had this happen on too many occasions that I began to look to the wisdom of herbal healers to find alternatives.

The ability to grow my own medicine has been an empowering experience even if I am only at the start of my learning and still only experimenting with the safest of medicinal plants. The designs, plants and recipes included here are ones I have found useful but if you are treating an illness, seek the advice of a qualified medicinal herbalist or your GP as I am not in a position to give medical advice.

Bites, cuts and stings are some of the most common ailments, especially for gardeners. I am a much more tentative pruner in the summer months having disturbed wasps nests on three separate occasions and I wish I had known then about the soothing properties of plantain for the many itchy days as the stings faded. I once had 30 stings on one leg after the ground gave way and my foot plunged into an underground nest. This design includes a selection of some of the most useful and easy to use herbs for first aid and information on how to use them. As with any plant that is new to you, test it out first by applying it in a small area somewhere known to be sensitive, such as the underside of your wrist. This way you should avoid any allergic reactions.

I have created a small tin of first aid equipment to use with the herbs for myself. This includes tweezers to remove splinters, small bandages to hold compresses and poultices in place and small drawstring bags to add herbs for making infusions. Some of the plants have been processed into balms and herbal oils and others dried and stored in airtight jars to provide a supply through the winter months when the garden is dormant. This way you can have a supply year round or have a handy medicine cabinet to take with you on your travels.

I designed the apothecary garden at Esholt Hall to have a mix of culinary and medicinal herbs as a useful resource for the community

Drying plantain leaves to store so I can make more balm or a poultice even in the depths of winter

Plant list

Cider gum (*Eucalyptus gunnii*) or snow gum (*Eucalyptus pauciflora* subsp. *Niphophila*)

Eucalyptus can grow to be a large evergreen tree but in this design it is coppiced, in spring, every other year to keep the plant small and to provide plenty of easy to reach foliage. Cut branches back every two years to the main trunk. Eucalyptus has white flowers in the summer but if you are coppicing it you are unlikely to get flowers as you will be cutting off the shoots where the flowers develop.

Eucalyptus has been used since ancient times to treat respiratory illnesses and you can harness this healing property by adding chopped leaves to a bowl of hot water for steam inhalation, where it acts as a decongestant and expectorant to clear mucus from the respiratory tracts.

It is one of the most powerful antiseptic herbs and can also be applied directly to the skin to clean wounds in the form of a compress or an infusion.

It prefers full sun and a sheltered position and when coppiced will be around 1.5m in height and 1.5m spread.

White willow (*Salix alba*)

White willow can grow to be a very large tree but, as with the eucalyptus, you can control the size by coppicing each year. It contains salicin which has anti-inflammatory and analgesic properties and is commonly used to reduce fever, treat skin inflammation, migraines and menstrual pains. Bark can be dried and made into a tincture to keep in your first aid kit. You can also make tea from the dried bark.

White willow prefers moist soil. It will grow more vigorously in full sun but will tolerate some shade. With yearly coppicing the height will be around 2m with a spread of 1-1.5m

Witch hazel (*Hamamelis virginiana*)

Witch hazel is a small tree which is grown for the medicinal properties of its bark and its small spider-like fragrant flowers in winter/spring. Its bark contains compounds with astringent and anti-inflammatory properties which are used to treat acne, psoriasis and eczema amongst other ailments. Witch hazel prefers a moist but well-drained soil in sun or part shade. It likes acidic soil but will tolerate most soils. It can grow to a height of around 6m but it is a fairly slow growing tree and you can prune it to keep it to your desired size.

Witch hazel has very pretty flowers and the scent is amazing in the depths of winter when not much else is flowering

Elderberry (*Sambucus nigra*)

Elder is a deciduous shrub that produces white flowers in spring and deep purple/black berries in autumn. If you want a crop of berries then don't harvest all the flowers as the flowers are the part that develop into the berries.

Elderberries are used to boost your immune system and are particularly helpful for viral infections like flu. Elderflowers can be used as a tea or syrup to relieve coughs and congestion associated with colds and flu. Both the flowers and berries can be used as a tincture or tea for pain relief and to reduce swelling.

Pruning is not necessary unless you want to control the size. You can cut elders back quite hard, right back to around 30cm from the ground, but you will lose the following year's flowers. You could use renewal pruning, which means cutting back one third of the oldest branches each year to as low as you can, leaving two thirds to flower and fruit. The following year some new growth will sprout up to replace the old branches you have removed. Elder will tolerate shade but will flower and fruit better in a sunny position. It can reach a height of around 3-4m and a spread of 2-3m.

You can use the native *Achillea millefolium* but there are cultivars such as this 'Pastel Mix' which add colour to your garden

Rosemary (*Salvia rosmarinus*)

Rosemary is a small evergreen shrub with very aromatic leaves and small purple or white flowers. You can eat young shoots, leaves and flowers raw or cooked. The leaves have a strong bitter flavour when eaten alone but blend well with other herbs in a tea. Rosemary is rich in volatile oils which are strongly antiseptic and anti-inflammatory. In herbal teas it can be effective for headaches, colds and anxiety and to improve your mood. An infusion of rosemary can be used as a hair wash to reduce dandruff and as an eyewash for infections. Pruning is not necessary other than to remove dead, diseased or dying branches.

Rosemary prefers a well-drained soil in full sun and is very drought resistant. There are many cultivars but most have a height and spread of around 1.5m.

Yarrow (*Achillea millefolium*)

Yarrow is a herbaceous perennial with flat flowerheads made up of many tiny flowers. It usually flowers in June to September and is a great plant for pollinators with its many tiny flower heads. Flower colour ranges from white to yellow to red. *Achillea* is named after Achilles, a hero in Greek mythology, who used it to heal his soldiers' wounds after the siege of Troy. It is very effective at stopping bleeding, even with deep wounds. It has many medicinal uses including treating wounds, fever, colds and flu, kidney disease and for menstrual pain. Fresh leaves can be crushed and applied directly to help relieve toothache. For bleeding, a spit poultice is best. Pick some leaves, chew them up a bit to release the juices then place on the wound.

Yarrow is pretty drought resistant and happy on poor and alkaline soil. It prefers sun but will tolerate some shade. It can grow to around 90cm tall on good soil or shorter if soil is poor or sandy, with a spread of around 45cm.

The native yarrow has white flowers which are much smaller than cultivated varieties

Lavender (*Lavandula angustifolia*)

Lavender is probably one of the most recognisable herbs. It is a small shrub with aromatic purple/blue flowers in the summer. It is well-known for its strong scent which is known to be calming. It also has anti-bacterial and antifungal effects. It can be used to treat bruises, burns and wounds and for relaxation. The most quick and easy way to use it is to rub a flower between your palms then inhale the volatile oils. You instantly feel calmer. Alternatively you can dry flowers to store for herbal tea, compresses and infusions or make a tincture. Flowers should be harvested just before the buds open and can be hung to dry out of direct sunlight.

Plants should be pruned just after the flowers have gone over, when they turn from purple to grey. They may produce a second flush of flowers and can be cut back again at the beginning of autumn. Do not cut past the lowest leaves as they will not resprout from old wood. Ideally cut back, leaving two sets of leaves. I like to do this final prune around March when the worst of the hard frosts are over. This way I can cut out any branches that have died off over the winter. Lavender needs a well-drained soil and full sun. Most grow to around 0.75-1m in height with around 50-75cm spread. Some varieties can be very compact and some form much larger mounds so choose a variety to fit your available space. They do not like competition from other plants so I tend to position them on the front edge of a border and give them plenty of space.

Pot marigold (*Calendula officinalis*)

Calendula is a fast growing annual or biennial which will happily self-seed all over your garden. It has bright orange daisy-like flowers and, if deadheaded, will flower right up until the first hard frosts. The leaves are also aromatic and can be used medicinally. The flowers are quite resinous and have potent healing properties. Calendula has traditionally been used as an anti-inflammatory, for skin conditions, to prevent infections and to promote wound healing. It is my favourite herb to experiment with at the moment. I have made a moisturiser using calendula-infused coconut oil and beeswax as a lifelong sufferer of acne. I have added it to herbal tea blends to try to tackle a chronic inflammation issue. It's such a beautiful herb to include in any planting scheme. Deadhead to prolong flowering. It usually self-seeds or you can easily save your own seed as seed heads are available to harvest over a long period. It is happy in sun or part shade and is drought tolerant. The height and spread are 10-50cm depending on how fertile the soil is and the availability of water.

Calendula are a vibrant addition to the garden and have powerful healing qualities too

It is a great plant to fill in any gaps in your perennial planting schemes.

Feverfew (*Tanacetum parthenium*)

Feverfew is a short-lived perennial in the daisy family. It is the white flowers, blooming in July and August, that are used. It is somewhat evergreen in mild winters. As its common name suggests, its historic use has been to treat fever. It can also be used to treat pain, relax spasms, improve digestion and it has a laxative effect. It is effective at relieving headaches and migraines. It can be applied externally to treat insect bites and bruising.

Feverfew self-seeds easily and can become a bit of a nuisance. It prefers sun and is tolerant of a wide range of conditions including exposed sites. When it is happy it can get to a height of 60cm and a spread of 40cm.

Feverfew growing with wormwood (silver feathery foliage) and burdock

Broadleaf plantain (*Plantago major*)

Plantain is a ground-hugging native herbaceous perennial. It is prized for the medicinal quality of its leaves although you can also eat the flowers and seeds.

The leaves are often used for their antihistamine, antifungal and analgesic qualities and are very effective on nettle stings and insect bites. I make a spit poultice from fresh leaves and lay them over bites and stings and it is very effective at reducing redness and irritation. Fresh leaves are usually available year round but you may want to dry some for your first aid kit to have some on hand. They can simply be dried and stored in an airtight container. It can be made into a tea to help with a cough. The seeds of plantain contain a mucilage which swells in the gut and acts as a laxative. This mucilage can also be very soothing to the gut.

Plantain is very tolerant of trampling and makes a good addition to a lawn or can be used between paving or as ground cover. It is happy in most conditions from soggy lawn to dry gravel so is a very easy plant to please. Its size depends on the ground conditions and whether it is being mown down in a lawn. Its height can be as short as 5cm in a lawn or up to 40cm if it's in rich soil with little competition. Spread is usually 10-35cm.

Thyme (*Thymus vulgaris*)

Thyme is a low growing evergreen shrubby herb. It flowers from June to August and is a great plant for pollinators. Thyme is valued for its antiseptic and antioxidant properties and can be used fresh all year round or dried for storage. I recently used thyme in a tea with honeysuckle for a sore throat and was amazed at how effective it was.

It is used to treat respiratory diseases and can be used as a deodorant, to destroy parasitic worms, as a disinfectant, for diarrhoea and for a variety of other ailments.

Thyme must have full sun and no competition. I struggle to keep it alive in my garden for more than a couple of years unless I plant it in a pot. If you have free draining soil you will probably have more luck. There are creeping varieties that grow less than 1cm in height but spread out to 50cm plus. The common thyme has a height of 30cm and a spread of 40cm.

Burdock (*Arctium lappa*)

Burdock is a biennial native herbaceous perennial. Its seed heads are the sticky buds that inspired the invention of velcro. It is a great herb for detoxifying the liver. The roots contain inulin, a type of prebiotic fibre, which is able to reduce inflammation in the gut. Its high fibre content helps to stimulate digestion and relieve constipation. Burdock is antifungal and antibacterial and the leaves can be used as a poultice on ulcers, burns and sores. You can wrap a cut in a burdock leaf instead of a bandage. They like a well-drained and ideally not compacted or rocky soil to ensure you get a good root harvest. The plants grow to a height of between 1-2m with a spread of around 1-1.5m. They have tall flower spikes in the second year.

Peppermint (*Mentha x piperita*)

Mint is a herbaceous perennial that spreads by rhizomes. Mint tea is often given after meals to aid digestion. It can also be used to ease fevers, for stomach aches, nausea and parasites. The leaves should be harvested when the plant is just coming into flower, and can be dried for later use. A poultice can be made from crushed leaves and used on bruises. The essential oil in the leaves is antiseptic and an infusion of the leaves can be used on wound treatments.

It can become invasive so ideally place a barrier around it to contain it. I often use a timber edge sunk about 10cm into the soil as the rhizomes run along or just below the soil surface. Plants benefit from lifting and dividing every couple of years or the vigour can deteriorate. Mint is happy in moist soil in the sun

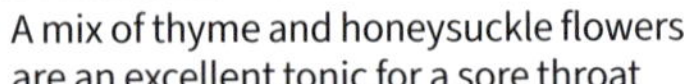

A mix of thyme and honeysuckle flowers are an excellent tonic for a sore throat

or shade. It will grow to around 1m tall and although I would describe the spread as indefinite without control measures, I would give it 0.5-1m in a design depending on how much of the top growth you will be harvesting.

Chamomile (*Chamaemelum nobile*)

Chamomile is a low growing perennial plant with small daisy-like flowers. It is the flowers that are used medicinally. It is well-known as a calming herb and I remember being given a cup of chamomile tea at bedtime as a child to help me sleep. It was used by Greek herbalists to treat fever. The flowers can be put in bags and soaked in hot water then cooled to use as compresses on the eyes to reduce inflammation. Bags of the flowers can be added to baths to help treat sunburn or rashes and to condition the hair. I still enjoy it as a tea almost daily and find it very refreshing. It is evergreen so just needs the dead stems removed if you want it to look tidy. Beware of the lawn chamomile variety 'Treneague' as this doesn't produce flowers. It is bred for its dense evergreen foliage. It grows to a height of around 25cm and spread of 30cm.

The variegated form of lemon balm gives a nice splash of yellow amongst the other green foliage and tastes just as delicious

Lemon balm (*Melissa officinalis*)

Lemon balm is a herbaceous perennial in the mint family. It has small white flowers in summer that have a high nectar content so are a great food source for pollinating insects. As the name suggests, the leaves have a strong lemony smell and have antimicrobial, antioxidant and anti-inflammatory properties. A tea made from the leaves can be uplifting and relieve tension headaches. It is often used to help people with insomnia and anxiety. It can become invasive and self-seeds freely in the right conditions so you may want to lift and divide your plant every few years. You can cut all the foliage right back to the ground once it has flowered and you will get a second flush of fresh leaves which can be used into the autumn. It is happy in most soils; you may want to give it a less fertile soil to help control its vigour. It grows to around 1m tall with a spread of 50-75cm.

Comfrey (*Symphytum officinale*)

Comfrey is a large herbaceous perennial which can get quite invasive. It is traditionally used to treat wounds, muscle and joint pains, fractures and osteoarthritis. It is well-known for being able to speed up and ensure proper healing of wounds. In fact I have read that you need to be sure you have cleaned a wound well before using it as it may trap dirt in as the skin heals over. Due to the discovery that it contains pyrrolizidine alkaloids, it is often recommended that it is only used externally as it could cause liver damage.

Comfrey is a large plant so give it plenty of room. It prefers a moist soil but I have grown it in fairly dry soil, it just grows less vigorously. It is happy in sun but will tolerate some shade. Its height and spread are 1.5m.

Arnica (*Arnica chamissonis*)

True arnica, *Arnica montana*, is not suited to the conditions in most of the UK as it is a mountainside plant from Europe and Siberia. North American arnica has the same healing properties but is much easier to grow here. It has yellow flowers in summer and into autumn. Arnica is used to treat sprains and bruises and for muscle aches, but is only to be used externally in a balm as it is poisonous to eat. It prefers a well-drained, sandy, slightly alkaline soil in semi-shade or in a sunny position. It grows to around 75cm tall with a spread of 50cm.

The leaves of lambs ears can be used as a natural plaster, simply lay them on your wound. They are absorbent and have antibacterial properties.

Self-heal or heal-all (*Prunella vulgaris*)

Self-heal is a low growing ground cover herbaceous perennial. It has deep purple flower spikes which are loved by pollinators. It is a native plant to the UK and, as its name suggests, it has a long history as a healing plant and has been reputed to heal almost any ailment from cuts and boils to diarrhea and cancer. Interestingly in Europe the flowers tend to be used when in bloom but in Chinese medicine they tend to use the flower-heads once they have finished flowering. It is often found in lawns where it grows flat to the turf but if found in the wild it can grow up to 40cm tall. It is not too fussy about soil type but seems to grow best in a moist soil. It tends to flower in spring but has a long flowering period. If grown in a lawn, it will continue to bloom for many months as it keeps being 'deadheaded' each time the lawn is cut.

Garlic (*Allium sativum*)

Garlic has been used by many ancient civilisations, such as in ancient Greece, Egypt, China and the Roman Empire. There is an increasing body of evidence which now backs up the medicinal claims from history. This research includes showing its immune-boosting properties and its ability to lower cholesterol and blood pressure. I remember my mum used to add a clove of garlic to warm olive oil and once cooled, she would put the clove of garlic and oil into my ear to cure earache. I am not suggesting you try this without professional advice but it seemed to work.

Garlic is traditionally grown as an annual crop, replanting a clove in autumn or spring to grow a new bulb but I grow it as a perennial plant. The cloves do not get as big but it means I have a constant supply in the garden. Garlic needs full sun to grow well and a well-drained soil to prevent the bulbs from rotting. Garlic grows to a height of 45cm but is a tall narrow plant with a spread of only 10cm so you can fit quite a few plants into a small space.

Many of these plants can be found growing in the wild and you start to notice them more and more as you learn how to identify them. I have picked plantain on many occasions on walks to soothe nettle or wasp stings. Even if you just add a couple of these plants into your existing garden, you can start to build up a collection of healing plants to use in emergencies.

Skin Care Garden

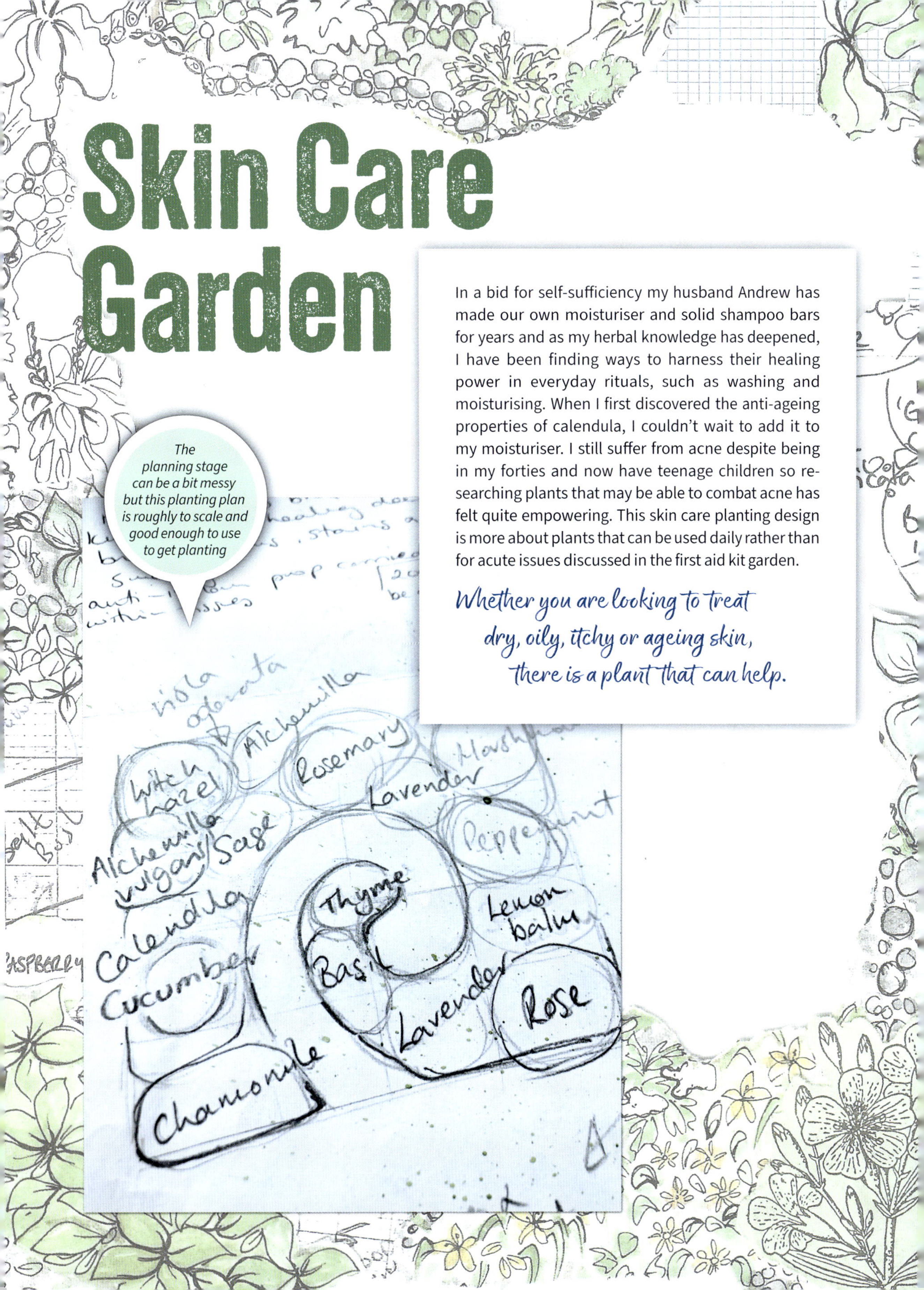

In a bid for self-sufficiency my husband Andrew has made our own moisturiser and solid shampoo bars for years and as my herbal knowledge has deepened, I have been finding ways to harness their healing power in everyday rituals, such as washing and moisturising. When I first discovered the anti-ageing properties of calendula, I couldn't wait to add it to my moisturiser. I still suffer from acne despite being in my forties and now have teenage children so researching plants that may be able to combat acne has felt quite empowering. This skin care planting design is more about plants that can be used daily rather than for acute issues discussed in the first aid kit garden.

Whether you are looking to treat dry, oily, itchy or ageing skin, there is a plant that can help.

Herbal oil infusion

The easiest way to extract a herb's healing properties is by making an infusion with herbs either in hot water or in oil. Choose your oil carefully as some can clog pores or be too greasy. I tend to use olive oil for balms and coconut and jojoba for my facial moisturiser but everyone's skin is different so you may want to experiment.

To make a simple balm

This starts by infusing the herbs in oil. The moisture in fresh herbs can cause the oil to spoil due to moulds so either dry your herbs first or as a minimum I would let them wilt for around 12 hours first. Fill a jar to within an inch of the rim with your chosen herb then pour in the oil to the top, making sure all the herbs are under the oil.

Place the jar on a sunny windowsill for a few weeks and let the heat of the sun speed up the extraction. Alternatively some herbs are better infused in the dark, this is why it pays to do your research first.

If you are in a hurry you can speed up the infusion process by heating the oil very gently on a bain marie. Find a bowl with a larger rim diameter than your pan. Fill the bowl with the oil and herbs and the pan with hot water. Place the bowl into the pan, ensuring it sits off the bottom of the pan but in the hot water. Keep the water hot on a low simmer for around two hours, checking and stirring the herbs and oil every now and again.

Once you have infused the oil, strain the oil either using a muslin cloth or coffee filter paper. It filters much more quickly through a cloth. You can use the oil as it is, especially for massage or to use as hair oil.

If you want to make a balm, take the strained oil and heat very gently as above and add in the beeswax or the vegan alternative, candelilla wax. The waxes are to set the liquid oil into a solid balm. As a general guide, use a ratio of one part beeswax to four or five parts oil or one part candelilla wax to eight or ten parts oil. You may want to experiment to get the right consistency for what you want. Some oils need more wax and some need less. Heat the oil very gently, just long enough for the wax to melt, then take off the heat and pour into a jar or small tin and leave to set. Importantly, don't forget to label it so you know what it is.

Infusing olive oil with calendula flowers ready to make a balm. I left the flowers in the oil for around 4-5 weeks before straining them.

Lavender and chamomile calming facial toner

Place a mix of lavender and chamomile flowers into a bowl or jar and pour over boiling water at a ratio of one part flowers to two parts water. I have some cup measures I like to use but you can use any cup or jar you have to hand to measure volume rather than weight. Cover the infusion to prevent the volatile oils from evaporating and leave until cool. Strain and pour into an airtight container or jar. You can store the toner in the fridge for up to five days and use as you would any toner, gently patting onto your skin using cotton wool or ideally a reusable washable cleansing pad.

You can experiment with different plants to see which are suited to your skin type. You can make the above recipes with almost any of the plants in the skin care garden. Just remember to do your research and test on a small area first before applying to a large patch of skin or your whole face.

Plan design for the skin care garden

Anti-ageing calendula and rose balm

Add an equal mix of calendula flower heads and rose petals to a jar and cover the herbs with jojoba oil. Jojoba oil is actually a wax so if you have had it stored in a cold room, you may need to warm it first to make it fully liquid. Either do a cold infusion over a few weeks or warm the oil on the stove as described above. Once the oil has been strained, warm it gently and melt in 10g beeswax (or 5g candelilla wax) for every 40g of infused oil. Pour into your chosen container and let it cool and set. This can be used daily.

I can't imagine being without calendula in my garden now I know of its amazing healing and anti-ageing properties although I do like to think that wrinkles give a certain look of wisdom as I get older, so let's hope it doesn't work too well!

Plant list and properties

The scope of this book is planting design. I have included some of the properties of the plants and ways to use them, but I am not a herbalist. I would suggest further research to make sure you are using them correctly.

Cucumber (*Cucumis sativus*)

Cucumber is hydrating, soothing and astringent. It can be sliced and placed on the skin or made into a purée as a face mask.

Chamomile (*Chamaemelum nobile*)

Antibacterial, antioxidant and anti-inflammatory, it is soothing and stimulates skin repair. Infused oils can be used in balms, or cold chamomile tea as a calming toner.

Pot marigold (*Calendula officinalis*)

Calendula is hydrating, anti-ageing, anti-microbial, heals wounds and treats nappy rash. Calendula-infused oil can be used in balms and moisturisers.

Lavender (*Lavandula angustifolia* or x *intermedia*)

Lavender is calming for the skin. It is antimicrobial, cleansing, anti-ageing, anti-acne and stimulates cell repair. It can be infused in oil and made into a balm or to add to moisturisers.

Marshmallow (*Althea officinalis*)

Marshmallow is cooling, protective and hydrating and is used to soften and condition skin. It can be used to thicken other formulas thanks to its mucilage. The root can be infused in oil for balms or the powdered root can be added to face masks.

Peppermint (*Mentha* x *piperita*)

Peppermint is cooling, cleansing, anti-microbial, anti-acne and stimulates blood flow. Mix chopped mint leaves into natural face masks for a refreshing feel. Make a mint infusion to use as a facial toner.

Rosemary (*Salvia rosmarinus*)

Rosemary is astringent, cleansing, anti-acne and anti-fungal. It can offer some protection from the damaging effects of the sun. Rosemary-infused oil can be used directly as a body oil or sprigs of rosemary can be added to hot water for a facial steam.

Thyme (*Thymus vulgaris*)

Thyme is cleansing, anti-acne and an astringent. Thyme boosts circulation and helps clear bacterial infections and inflammation. Mix crushed thyme with honey to make a face mask or infuse in hot water, allow to cool and wipe onto your skin as a facial toner.

Violet (*Viola odorata*)

Viola is soothing and cleansing. Its flowers and leaves contain mucilage which can soothe irritated skin. Infuse the flowers and leaves to create body oil. Add dried

Harvesting marshmallow flowers to dry for later use

Alchemilla mollis and *A. vulgaris* can be used interchangeably in recipes. If you have an *Alchemilla* in your garden, it is most likely to be *A. mollis*.

I like to harvest and dry plantain leaves when they are plentiful so I can store them. Both broadleaf plantain (*Plantago major*) and ribwort plantain (*P. lanceolata* pictured here) can be used interchangeably in skin care.

Any rose petals can be used for your skin care but some will be more potent than others

or fresh flowers to a small muslin bag and add to the bath for a calming effect on the skin.

Lady's mantle (*Alchemilla mollis*)

Alchemilla can tighten pores and reduce inflammation. It is soothing, astringent and cleansing. An infused oil can be used on its own as a body oil or made into a body butter.

Ribworth plantain (*Plantago lanceolata*)

Plantain leaves have wonderful soothing qualities so are great as an everyday herb. They are anti-inflammatory so useful for those who suffer from acne and other types of skin inflammation.

Rose (*Rosa gallica* var. *officinalis* is the apothecary's rose)

Any rose can be used, it just may not have the potency of the apothecary's rose.

Rose is soothing, hydrating, mildly astringent and anti-acne. Mix petals with honey to make a face mask or infuse petals in oil to make a soothing skin balm.

Witch hazel (*Hamamelis virginiana*)

Witch hazel is astringent, anti-inflammatory and cleansing. Used as a toner, it removes oils and tightens pores. The bark is boiled in distilled water to make an astringent.

Herbal Tea Garden

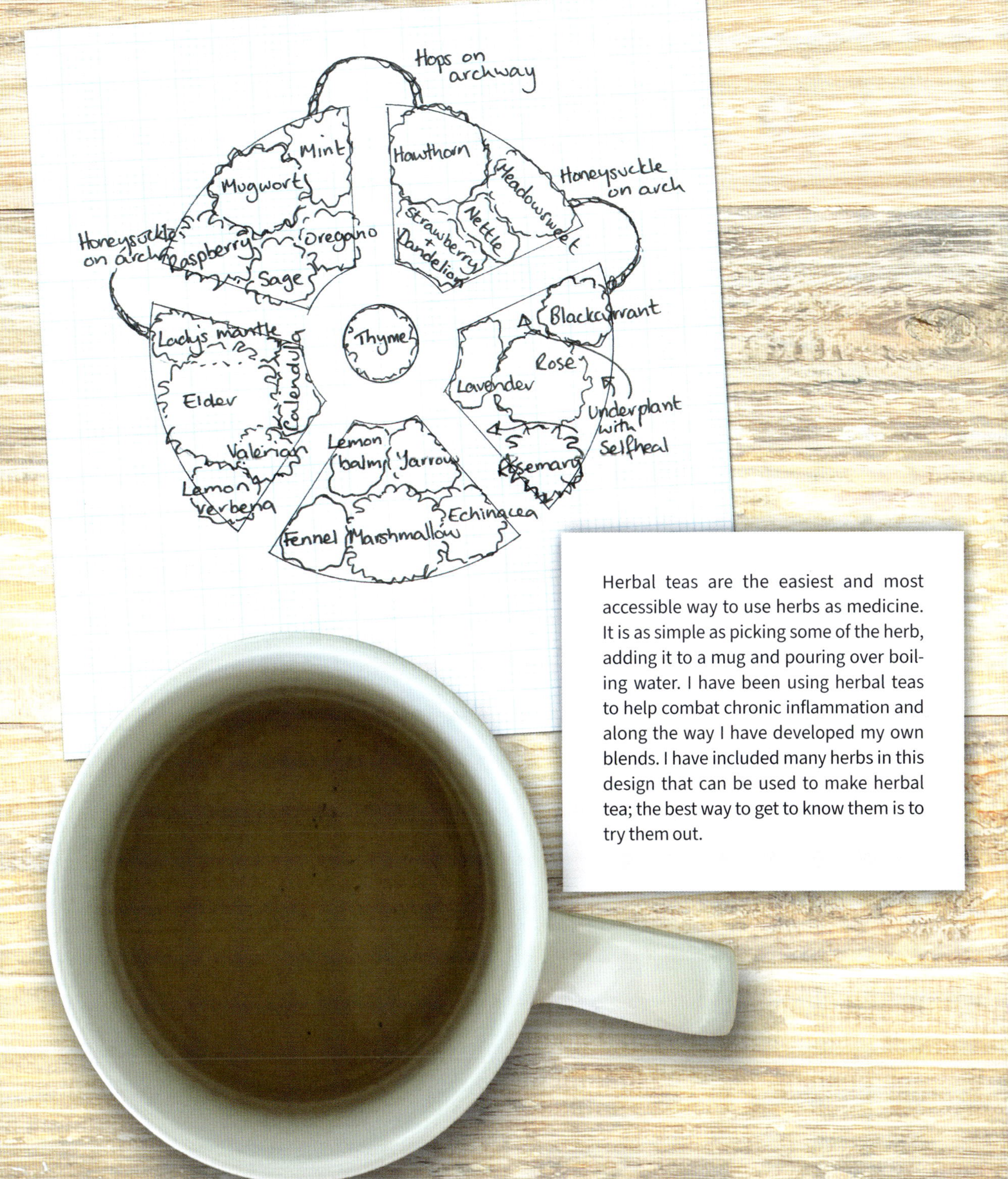

Herbal teas are the easiest and most accessible way to use herbs as medicine. It is as simple as picking some of the herb, adding it to a mug and pouring over boiling water. I have been using herbal teas to help combat chronic inflammation and along the way I have developed my own blends. I have included many herbs in this design that can be used to make herbal tea; the best way to get to know them is to try them out.

Blending herbal teas

In terms of using them for healing, I found herbs that have similar properties and combined them. For sore throats I use thyme and honeysuckle as both have anti-viral and antiseptic properties. The thyme by itself was not to my taste but I quite enjoy it with honeysuckle.

To help relax I combine chamomile, lavender and lemon balm. Spend some time finding herbs you enjoy drinking. There is usually more than one herb you could use for an ailment, or just to maintain health, so try to find the one you prefer as this will make it much more likely that you will drink it. To save time, you can prepare a large jug of your herbal tea which you can keep in the fridge for up to three days. You can then either reheat it or add ice and enjoy it as iced tea.

To find a nice flavour mix, I like to make a pot of each individual herbal tea then pour different combinations into a mug to try. If I don't like something, I can easily try another blend.

Two types of thyme growing with alpine strawberries. The strawberries were too invasive so they had to come out the following year.

Cover your cup when making herbal tea so that you don't lose their healing compounds via evaporation. I love this mushroom mug with its own lid but I often use a small side plate which does the same job.

As an example, start with one herb, such as chamomile. Pour in some mint tea and try the combination. If you like it, add in something else, such as lavender. If you don't like the addition of lavender, start again with chamomile and mint but now try another herb like rose petals. Keep going until you have a blend you like. Now you can take the dried herbs you have selected and mix them together in a jar so you have the tea ready blended.

Each herb has different levels of potency so check on the recommended dose. As a rule of thumb I tend to use 1-2 teaspoons of dried herb or herbal blend per cup, or a few sprigs/3 tsp equivalent of fresh herb. You can add a lot more fresh mint to a mug than fresh rosemary or thyme. Some teas are made from the root, some from the stem and leaves and some from the flowers, so check which part of the plant you are meant to use before preparing your tea.

With your herbal tea garden planting, you may find over time that you require a lot of one type of herb and only a small amount of another so you can adapt your design and make room for more of your well used herbs and maybe even remove some of the herbs you don't use at all. However I do think it can be helpful to have a herb in the garden even if you haven't found a need for it yet; you never know when it may be the herb you need.

Plant list for the herbal tea garden

Blackcurrant (*Ribes nigrum*)

A tea can be made from the fruits or leaves or a combination of both. Use of blackcurrant in herbal medicine dates back to medieval times. A 2014 study showed that extracts from the leaves had anti-viral properties and could help prevent flu and viral colds. The leaves and fruits are high in vitamin C and other antioxidants, helping to boost the immune system and with the repair and growth of new cells.

Chamomile (*Chamaemelum nobile*)

Calming, promotes sleep, aids digestion, calms muscle cramps, relieves headaches and reduces menstrual cramps.

Dandelion (*Taraxacum officinale*)

Two different drinks can be made from dandelions. A tea is made from the flowers and leaves and a coffee substitute can be made from the roasted roots. Both have similar healing properties but the leaves have more diuretic compounds than the roots and tend to be used to reduce bloating and to eliminate excess water from the body. The roots can improve liver and gall-bladder functions, increase appetite and aid digestion.

Dwarf hops (*Humulus lupulus*)

'Sovereign', 'Prima Donna' and 'Herald' are all dwarf varieties of hop. Hops have a sedative effect and are useful for treating anxiety, sleep disorders and restless legs syndrome. The tea stimulates the digestive system if taken before a meal.

Echinacea (*Echinacea purpurea, E. pallida, E. angustifolia*)

The most common uses of echinacea are for boosting the immune system and to help reduce symptoms from the common cold. The anti-inflammatory properties help to reduce swelling, irritation and sore throats. The roots and flowers are most commonly used but you can also use the leaves and the stems to make tea.

Elderflower or berry (*Sambucus nigra*)

Both berries and flowers can be used to make tea and both have similar properties for strengthening the immune system, fighting the flu virus and aiding digestion.

Fennel (*Foeniculum vulgare*)

The seeds are used to make a tea with many health benefits. The seeds have antispasmodic properties that make it useful in treating irritable bowel syndrome and aiding digestion. It also helps the body to absorb iron and aids breast milk production.

Hawthorn (*Crataegus monogyna*)

The benefits of this brew of the flowers, leaves and berries are mostly for heart health. Hawthorn tea helps to strengthen the heart muscle, increase blood flow and lower blood pressure.

Hops can climb up any trellis or structure you already have or you can build your own obelisk

I harvest honeysuckle for drying over several weeks, taking my colander out each week to see which flowers are looking open but not fading

Honeysuckle (*Lonicera periclymenum* and *L. japonica*)

Traditionally it has been used to help fight infections from the common cold because it is anti-viral, antibacterial and anti-inflammatory and also helps to treat headaches. It is said to reduce the symptoms of arthritis and has anti-aging properties.

Lady's mantle (*Alchemilla mollis*)

This tea may help to regulate the menstrual cycle, reduce excessive menstrual bleeding and help to manage menopausal symptoms.

Lavender (*Lavandula angustifolia, L. x intermedia*)

This tea improves sleep quality, reduces stress and is a natural antidepressant.

Lemon balm (*Melissa officinalis*)

The most well-known benefits of lemon balm tea are to aid sleep and reduce anxiety. It is a very calming tea.

Lemon verbena (*Aloysia citrodora*)

It is a very calming tea and is useful in treating anxiety and insomnia. It has been used historically to treat digestive complaints and respiratory illness.

Marshmallow (*Althea officinalis*)

The mucilage in marshmallow coats the digestive tract with a calming coating so is beneficial for digestive complaints and repairing the gut lining. It is antibacterial and useful for sore throats, coughs and urinary tract infections.

Meadowsweet (*Filipendula ulmaria*)

The leaves and flowers can be used in tea and contain small amounts of salicylic acid, a precursor to aspirin. It can be used to help alleviate joint pain and arthritis. It can help to reduce heartburn and stomach ulcers. It also acts as a diuretic which makes it useful in the treatment of urinary tract infections and kidney infections.

Lavender and linden flowers ready to be dried to make tea

Mint (*Mentha* sp.) peppermint (*M. x piperita*), apple mint (*M. suaveolens*), spearmint (*M. spicata*), Swiss mint (*M. x piperita* 'Swiss'), lavender mint (*M. piperita f. citrata* 'Lavender')

Each mint has its own unique flavour but all have similar health benefits, particularly in treating stomach ache, nausea and vomiting. Mint calms the spasms in the muscles lining the gut. It is also an effective decongestant, may relieve the pain of osteoarthritis and lower blood sugar levels.

Mugwort (*Artemisia vulgaris*)

Traditionally mugwort has been used to help ease digestive troubles and bloating. It is said to help you to remember dreams and to reduce anxiety. It is mainly the leaves that are used to make tea. The leaves contain high levels of potassium, calcium and iron and may help prevent osteoporosis. The active compounds in mugwort are quite powerful so use sparingly; it has been said to cause hallucinations.

Mint can start to take over a bed if you don't restrict its roots

Variegated oregano adds a bit of interest to the border and the flavour is very similar to the wild form

Nettle (*Urtica dioica*)

Nettles have powerful healing properties and give the immune system a boost. Historically nettle tea has been used to help relieve painful muscles and inflammation and may help reduce pain associated with osteo-arthritis. It can also be used to help flush out harmful bacteria associated with urinary tract infections.

Oregano (*Origanum vulgare*)

It is anti-inflammatory and can help to improve respiratory health, aid digestion, help with weight loss and boost your immune system.

Pot marigold (*Calendula officinalis*)

Calendula is rich in antioxidants which can help prevent cell damage and fight oxidative stress. It has traditionally been used to treat digestive complaints thanks to its

Calendula is a very healing herb but it does have a slightly bitter flavour in a tea

Sage growing with *Buddleja* and *Phacelia* in a community garden

anti-inflammatory qualities. It may even fight certain cancer cells but more research is needed.

Raspberry leaf (*Rubus idaeus*)

This tea is said to help tighten muscles in the pelvic region and the uterus which can make childbirth less painful and may lower the chances of complications during labour. It is also very nutritious.

Rose petals (*Rosa* sp.)

A study (Rose petal tea as an antioxidant rich beverage, 2006) found rose petal tea to have antioxidant activity and phenol content that is equal to or higher than green tea. It found the cultivars with the highest levels to be *Rosa* 'San Francisco', *R.* 'Katharina Zeimet', *R.* 'Mercedes' and *R. damascena*. In Chinese medicine, *Rosa rugosa* is the rose of choice and historically in the UK, *Rosa gallica* var. *officinalis* has been used.

Rosemary (*Salvia rosmarinus*)

Improved memory is one benefit of rosemary tea. It is said to protect your brain health and improve your mood. It may also offer protection for your vision and eye health. There is research into its anti-tumour properties (Supercritical fluid extracts of rosemary leaves exhibit potent anti-inflammation and anti-tumour effects, 2007).

Sage (*Salvia officinalis*)

Sage tea is rich in antioxidants and anti-inflammatory compounds. It can be used to treat pain and inflammation in the mouth, for sore throats and bad breath. It may help improve brain health and reduce the likelihood of brain-related disease such as Alzheimer's.

Self-heal (*Prunella vulgaris*)

Self-heal has a high level of antioxidants and anti-viral properties. Its leaves and flowers can be used to help treat inflammation, headaches, sore throats, cold sores and complications associated with diabetes.

Strawberry (*Fragaria vesca* and *F. x ananassa*)

Any strawberry variety can be used but flavour will vary. Strawberry leaves are high in iron and its tea can help treat anaemia. It has a high antioxidant content which can neutralise harmful free radicals in the body. There is a long list of potential health benefits including helping with weight loss, improving heart health and reducing blood sugar levels.

Thyme (*Thymus vulgaris*)

Thymol, a compound in thyme, is an antiseptic. Thyme tea can be used as a mouthwash to treat mouth ulcers, bad breath and sore throats. It has broncho-dilating properties making it useful for treating respiratory conditions. It can also reduce bloating and flatulence.

Valerian (*Valeriana officinalis*)

The root of this plant is used to make the tea. It has a calming and sedative effect making it useful for insomnia and for reducing anxiety. It can also be used to treat migraines and headaches and for menstrual cramps.

Yarrow (*Achillea millefolium*)

This herb is thought to be one of the first herbs used as a medicine as it has been used for thousands of years. It has a huge list of health benefits. It can be used to treat irritable bowel syndrome and stomach ulcers. It is said to protect the heart, improve the immune system, reduce anxiety and improve liver function.

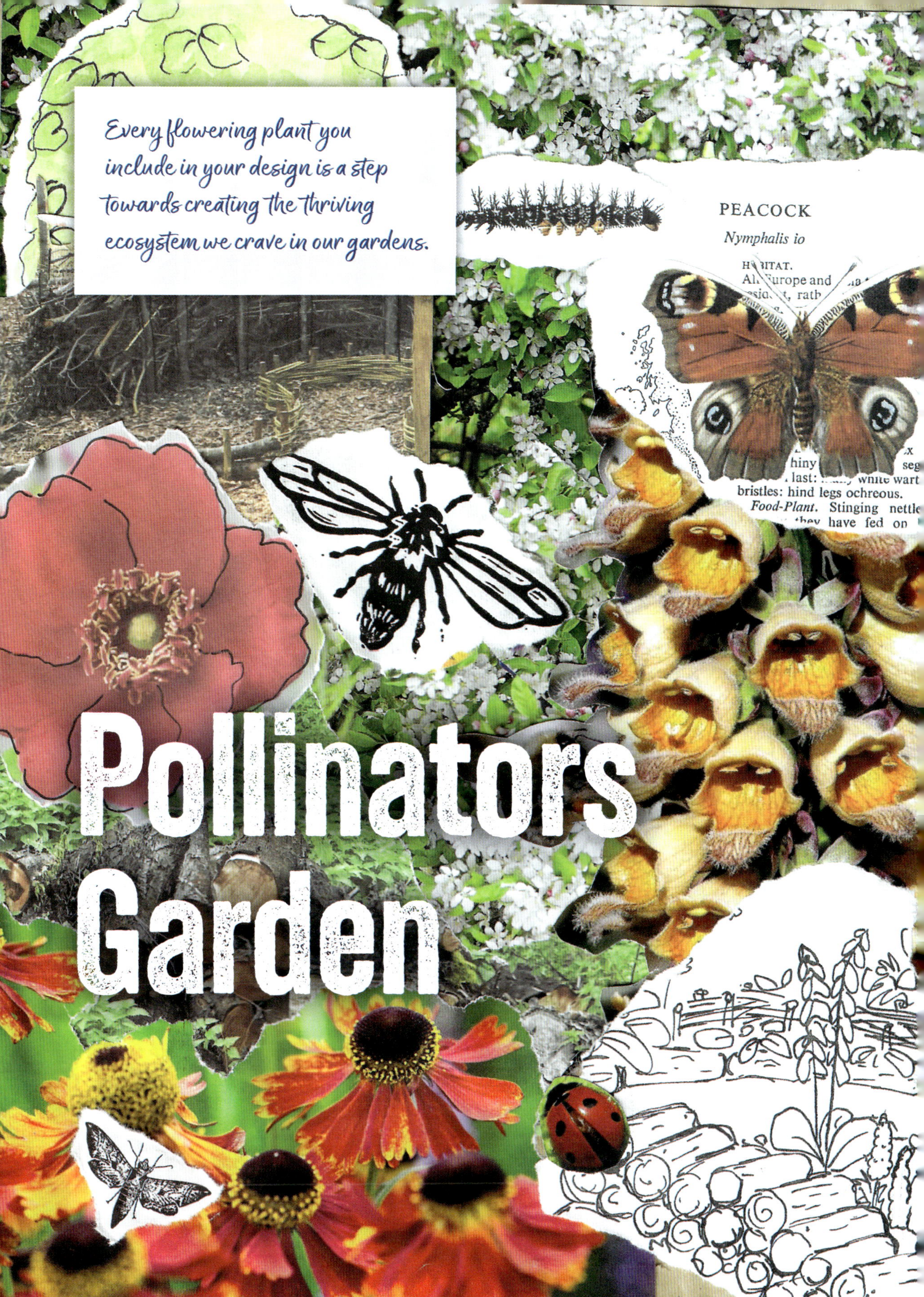
Every flowering plant you include in your design is a step towards creating the thriving ecosystem we crave in our gardens.
PEACOCK
Nymphalis io
bristles: hind legs ochreous.
Food-Plant. Stinging nettle
Pollinators Garden

Why it's important

Pollinators play a hugely important and vastly underestimated role in our delicate ecosystems. They are vital for the reproduction of many plants both in our natural wild spaces where they are a crucial part of the food web and for farmed plants to support humans. There are multiple threats to pollinators putting many ecosystems at risk. These threats are from habitat loss, poisoning from pesticides, herbicides and fungicides, both in farming and home gardens, and climate change. Whilst we may not easily be able to influence the above, we can provide a sanctuary in our own gardens and community spaces by providing food and shelter to as diverse a range of insects as possible.

Often when we talk of pollinators, we think of bees and butterflies and forget the vast range of other insects such as wasps, moths, flies and beetles. Many pollinators such as hoverflies have other important ecosystem roles, such as pest control by eating aphids. Even within the bee family, there are tree bees, wool carder bees, ground-nesting bees and honey bees to name just a few. Each insect has different needs in terms of food source but also habitat, breeding sites and some, such as red admiral butterflies, need specific host plants such as nettles for their larva. I have to be especially careful when harvesting calendula in the garden as there are always hoverflies swarming around the plants. This is why it is important to never strip a plant of its flowers when harvesting. I like to take no more than 50% to ensure I have left plenty of nourishing food for the pollinators.

Snowdrops are some of the first plants to emerge in the new year and are often visited by bees on a warm winter's day

Even our workplaces can provide valuable sources of pollen and nectar

Principles of a pollinator garden design

The best way to meet the needs of as many pollinators as possible is to have a wide diversity of plants for pollinators both in terms of flowering plants but also larva host plants. This goes for habitat also. Use flowers with a diversity of shapes. Foxgloves, *Digitalis* species, have bell-shaped flowers that allow bumble bees to land easily and rest while feeding. Yarrow, *Achillea* species, have many flowers arranged to form a large plate-like platform enabling insects to feed from numerous flowers without having to move far.

Different colours attract different pollinators so having a wide variety of colours will attract the most diverse range of pollinators. I always aim to have at least one plant flowering in each month of the year, no matter how small my planting plan. Longevity of season of available

Log piles are valuable habitat for hibernating and breeding

A small bug box can be used to provide habitat in a small garden

flowers means there will always be a food source available, especially on those warm winter days when brave insects are venturing out, food can be scarce as most plants are dormant. It is relatively easy to provide plants for pollinators from mid-spring until autumn. Winter is more of a challenge.

In winter, flowering plants provide a much needed source of nectar and pollen during the colder months. Examples of winter-flowering plants: *Crocus vernus*, early daffodils (*Narcissus* sp.), snowdrops (*Galanthus* sp.), winter aconites (*Eranthis hyemalis*), Oregon grape (*Mahonia aquifolium*), winter-flowering honeysuckle (*Lonicera fragrantissima*), primrose (*Primula vulgaris*), *Viburnum tinus*, witch hazel (*Hamamelis* sp.), hellebores (*Helleborus* sp.), ivy (*Hedera helix*).

Habitat is just as important. Providing a food source is just one piece of the puzzle. Pollinators have other needs, just as we do, for shelter and somewhere to breed. My main advice is, don't be too tidy. Leave stems standing over winter to provide snug places for insects to hibernate and shelter from winter weather. Build log piles as many insects lay eggs in cracks and crevices or even rotting wood. Some hoverflies and other insects need water to complete their life cycle. This doesn't need to be a big pond. Include a small pond or even just a bowl of water in your garden and make sure it is kept topped up with rainwater. The chemicals in tap water can kill insect larva. Place some small rocks or pebbles around the edge so insects can easily land and access the water source without falling in and drowning.

Flowers for different types of pollinators

Moths

Evening primrose (*Oenothera biennis*), honeysuckle (*Lonicera periclymenum*), white campion (*Silene latifolia*), sweet rocket (*Hesperis matronalis*), globe artichoke (*Cynara cardunculus*), lady's bedstraw (*Galium verum*).

Host plants for moth caterpillars

Mullein (*Verbascum thapsus*), mint (*Mentha* sp.), hazel (*Corylus avellana*), oak (*Quercus robur*), holly (*Ilex aquifolium*) and hawthorn (*Crataegus monogyna*).

Butterflies

Buddleia sp., *Verbena bonariensis*, *Echinacea* sp., lavender (*Lavandula* sp.), marjoram (*Origanum* sp.), globe thistle (*Echinops* sp.), *Rudbeckia* sp., *Sedum* sp. and *Hylotelephium* sp.

Host plants for butterfly caterpillars

Garlic mustard (*Alliaria petiolata*), lady's smock (*Cardamine pratensis*), birds foot trefoil (*Lotus corniculatus*), alder (*Alnus glutinosa*), buckthorn (*Frangula alnus*), nettle (*Urtica dioica*), nasturtium (*Tropaeolum officinale*).

Bees

Borage (*Borago officinalis*), *Salvia* sp., lavender (*Lavandula* sp.), bee balm (*Monarda* sp.), catmint (*Nepeta* sp.), *Crocus* sp., sunflowers (*Helianthus annuus*), sedum (*Hylotelephium* sp. and *Sedum* sp.), lungwort (*Pulmonaria officinalis*), chive.

Hoverflies

Rudbeckia sp., *Helenium* sp., fennel (*Foeniculum vulgare*), wild carrot (*Daucus carota*), coriander (*Coriandrum sativum*), yarrow (*Achillea millefolium*), meadowsweet (*Filipendula ulmaria*), ragged robin (*Lychnis flos-cuculi*), *Eupatorium* sp., asters (*Aster* sp., *Eurybia* sp.), *Hebe* sp., pot marigold (*Calendula officinalis*).

Pollen beetles

Roses (*Rosa* sp.), pumpkin, marrow and courgette (all three are *Cucurbita pepo*), ox-eye daisy (*Leucanthemum vulgare*), daffodil (*Narcissus* sp.), sweet peas (*Lathyrus odoratus*).

Rudbeckia add colour to the garden as well as being popular with butterflies

Bees love chives. I sat for ages watching many different types of bumblebee visit a patch of chives.

Natives versus non-natives

When discussing ecosystem design to encourage insects I find I am often asked about my opinion on the debate of native versus exotic (non-native) plants. Many feel it is important to include predominantly British native wild flowers and plants. I have always argued that using non-native species helps to extend the flowering season for pollinators. Helpfully the Royal Horticultural Society has undertaken research to help answer this question. The results conclude that natives are preferred by the herbivores who eat leaves. This includes caterpillars, aphids, weevils, leaf-mining flies, bees and gall wasps amongst others. They also concluded non-natives play a role in prolonging the flowering period for pollinators.

The conclusion was that non-natives support 20% fewer insects than natives, although other studies have shown no difference. My advice would be to include a mix of both natives and non-natives as this will give you the benefits of both. This could include a mixed hedge of native trees and shrubs such as beech, hazel, field maple and hawthorn surrounding your pollinator border, or including some native flowers into your planting scheme. Cultivated varieties of plants with double flowers or flowers bred for extra petals (most of the modern roses) should be avoided as these extra petals can prevent pollinators from getting to the nectar.

Native flowers suitable for your borders

Foxgloves (*Digitalis purpurea*), wild rose (*Rosa canina*), meadowsweet (*Filipendula ulmaria*), primrose (*Primula vulgaris*), bugle (*Ajuga reptans*), yarrow (*Achillea millefolium*), snakes head fritillary (*Fritillaria meleagris*), bellflower (*Campanula glomerata*), betony (*Stachys officinalis*) and hemp agrimony (*Eupatorium cannabinum*).

Hawthorn is a wonderful native flowering small tree often used as hedging in British gardens

Native plants for a hedge

Crab apples (*Malus sylvestris*) and hawthorn (*Crataegus monogyna*)

The flowers are good for pollinators and the fruit is loved by blackbirds.

Field maple (*Acer campestre*)

The flowers are good for pollinators. The fruit is eaten by birds and the leaves also attract aphids and the predators who eat them like ladybirds, hoverflies and birds.

Hazel (*Corylus avellana*) and oak (*Quercus robur*)

The leaves are food for herbivores.

Holly (*Ilex aquifolium*)

Evergreen plants are important for shelter in winter. The berries are loved by birds.

Prolonging the flowering season

There are a few other techniques you can use in the garden to prolong the availability of pollen and nectar. Deadheading flowers can encourage them to continue to produce more flowers. This is especially true of plants such as dahlias, roses and sweet peas. Another technique is to delay flowering by carrying out something called the 'Chelsea chop' which involves cutting back the foliage of a plant near to flowering time, usually in late May around the time of the Chelsea Flower Show. If you have two of the same plant and cut one back, this will mean you get a flush of flowers on the plant you haven't cut back. Just as the flowering is coming to an end, the plant you 'Chelsea chopped' should now be coming into flower.

Other plants, such as some of the older varieties of hardy geraniums, salvias and catmint, can be cut back entirely just as they have finished flowering and produce a second flush of flowers a few weeks later. It can seem a bit brutal in the height of summer but with a bit of a liquid feed, they will soon bounce back and provide many more weeks of flowers.

When designing this pollinator garden I split the year into individual months and make sure I have added at least one plant in each month. This is an easy way to make sure you have a constant supply of pollen and nectar through the year.

Flat-headed flowers such as fennel provide a nice landing pad for insects to rest on while feeding

Simple projects you can complete in a couple of hours

Within your current garden there are a few simple things you can do to make them more pollinator friendly. You could choose just one or add the whole list. If you make positive additions to your garden and share this achievement with a friend or neighbour, you can start to make changes on a wider scale.

1. Build a bug hotel. These can be as simple as a bundle of sticks stuffed into a tin can or a large scale purpose built box with many different types of natural materials included. My advice would be to start small and keep adding more over time. You can buy habitat boxes for specific insects, such as mason bees or ladybirds.

2. Rather than a 'hotel' you could simply make a log or stone pile or dead hedge in your garden. This is very simple and if you don't have any wood, you can ask around and see if anyone has dead branches destined for the tip that you could clear away for them.

3. Add some winter-flowering plants. During the summer months there is usually a good supply of food for insects. Adding a few winter-flowering plants can help to even out the availability.

4. Start your own insect observation diary; try to log and identify insects. One way to truly celebrate the amazing diversity of insect life in the garden is to get out there and see what you can find. You will very quickly discover the huge variety of shapes and colours you hadn't noticed before. There are some fantastic identification apps you can put on your phone or buy yourself an insect ID pocket book.

A log pile feature can be a great way to tidy up your garden or help a friend to get rid of some unwanted branches

A simple pond can be made by digging a hole then lining it with sand and then a pond liner

Pile rocks or logs around your pond to make it look more natural and to provide some cover for creatures accessing the pond

Planting plan for the pollinators garden

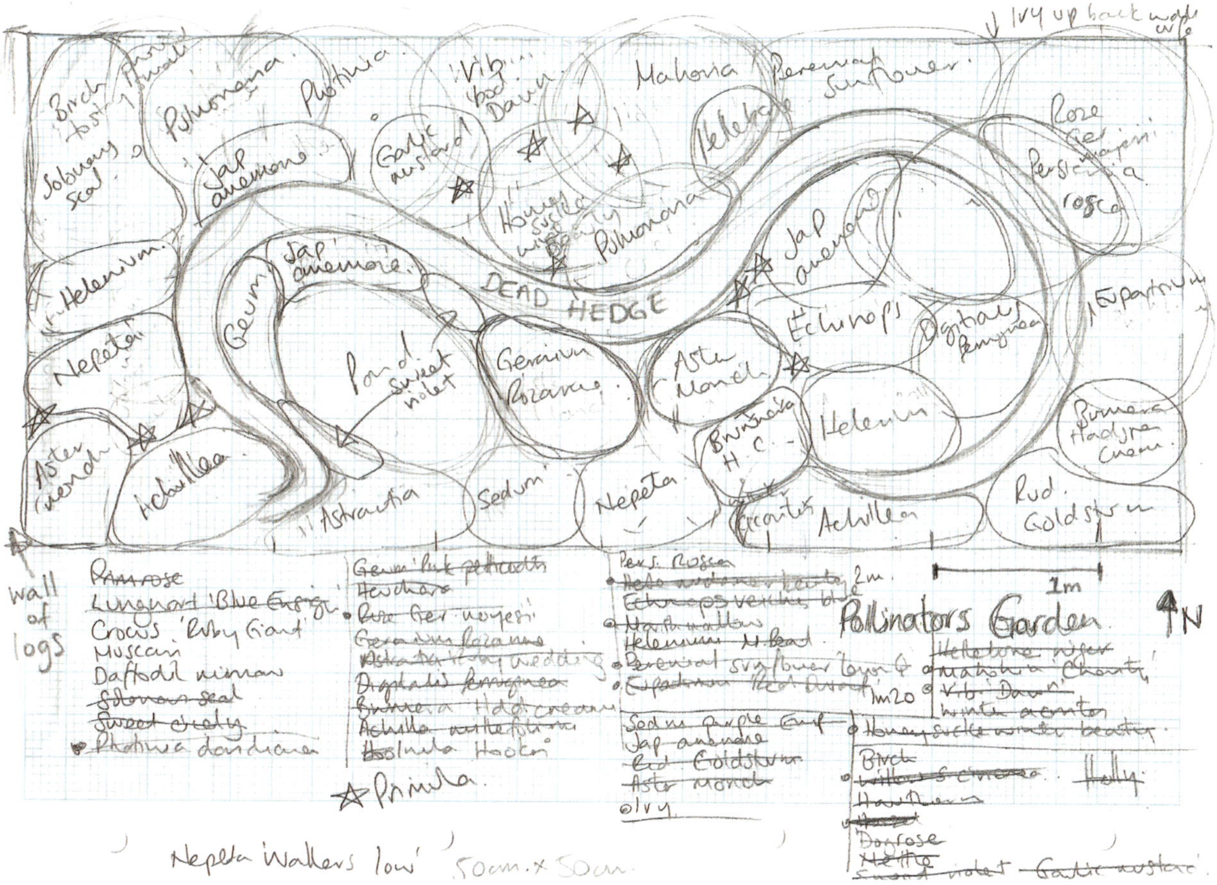

Key takeaways

- Try to achieve a year round supply of pollen and nectar
- Provide a source of water, however small
- Use pesticide free/organic gardening methods
- Try to include host plants for caterpillars
- Provide habitat such as log or leaf piles and dead hedges

Inula hookeri is popular with both bees and butterflies

Pollinator garden plant list

Spring

Brunnera macrophylla 'Hadspen Cream'
Dwarf daffodil 'Minnow' (*Narcissus*)
Grape hyacinth (*Muscari armeniacum*)
Lungwort 'Blue Ensign' (*Pulmonaria angustifolia*)
Primrose (*Primula vulgaris*)
Solomon seal (*Polygonatum* x *hybridum*)
Spring-flowering crocus 'Ruby Giant' (*Crocus tommasianus*)
Stransvaesia (*Photinia davidiana*)

Summer

Achillea millefolium 'Summer Pastels'
Catmint 'Walker's Low' (*Nepeta racemosa*)
Geranium 'Rozanne'
Geum 'Pink Petticoats'
Masterwort 'Ruby Wedding' (*Astrantia major*)
Rose 'Geranium' (*Rosa moyesii*)
Rusty foxglove (*Digitalis ferruginea*)

Late summer

Eupatorium 'Red Dwarf' (*Eupatorium maculatum* Atropurpureum group)
Globe thistle 'Veich's Blue' (*Echinops ritro*)
Perennial sunflower 'Lemon Queen' (*Helianthus* sp.)
Red bistort 'Rosea' (*Persicaria amplexicaulis*)
Sneezeweed 'Moerheim Beauty' (*Helenium* sp.)

Autumn

Aster 'Monch' (*Aster* x *frikartii*)
Ivy (*Hedera helix*)
Japanese anemone 'Robustissima' (*Anemone* x *hybrida*)
Rudbeckia 'Goldsturm' (*Rudbeckia fulgida* var. *sullivantii*)
Sedum 'Purple Emperor' (*Hylotelephium telephium* Atropurpureum group)

Geranium 'Rozanne' flowers for several months making it one of the best plants for pollinators. This also means it provides months of colour in the garden too.

Winter

Christmas rose (*Helleborus niger*)
Honeysuckle 'Winter Beauty' (*Lonicera* x *purpusii*)
Oregon grape 'Charity' (*Mahonia* x *media*)
Snowdrop (*Galanthus nivalis*)
Winter aconite (*Eranthis hyemalis*)

Insect host plants

Birch (*Betula pendula*) and willow (*Salix cinerea*) – host to several moth species and other wildlife
Garlic mustard (*Alliaria petiolata*) – host plant for small white butterflies
Sweet violet (*Viola odorata*) – larval host plant of fritillaries

Craft Garden

There are many crafts for which we can grow our own materials, including weaving, cordage, natural dyes and dried flowers

Weaving

Weaving materials can be foraged from the wild from hedgerows and in woodlands but you can grow many of these plants in your own garden for better access and quality. Willow is the plant most commonly grown in the UK for basket making. There are many different species and cultivated varieties depending on the colour, size and durability you are after. Smaller, finer willows such as 'Dicky Meadows' and 'Green Dicks' are used for fine basketry work.

I remember a story from a basketry apprentice that he wasn't allowed to use the variety 'Dicky Meadows' whilst learning, as it was too good to waste on beginners. When learning a new craft, I think it's wise to use the best quality you can grow. Nothing is more frustrating than trying to weave a basket from a hedgerow foraged willow which keeps snapping and kinking. In contrast, it is a real pleasure to weave with a pliable, fine basketry cultivar, giving a neat and strong finish. That said I also enjoy making a rustic style basket from foraged materials such as blackberry stems, honeysuckle, hedgerow hazel and lime suckers.

Weaving bird houses from a mix of materials such as willow and conifers

I use willow extensively in the garden for everything from woven bed edging, to living willow domes, obelisks, archways and plant labels. They are not very long lasting as structures; my bed edges usually last around 2-3 years which I don't mind as I love an excuse to reweave them and it also leaves flexibility for changes to the shape of beds and the position of pathways. Obelisks usually last about the same amount of time and I often weave them to sit as sculptural elements rather than to support plants; this shows off their construction.

If you are growing plants that are new to you or in a community setting where it is important to correctly identify plants for beginners, you can make your own wooden plant labels. Gather lengths of willow, hazel or whatever straight branches you have with roughly 3cm diameter, cut or whittle to a point at one end; use a knife or potato peeler to strip the bark off one face of the other end to create a relatively flat face to write on. I have tried pencil and permanent marker but both fade fairly quickly. I have found that paint markers last much longer, especially if you give the peeled face a coat of varnish or beeswax after writing the text. Pyrography is even longer lasting and looks more natural; this uses heat to burn a line into the wood using a tool similar to a soldering iron.

Hazel is a fantastic tree to coppice for bean poles and pea sticks. In a small garden it can be difficult to fit in more than one tree. If you can fit in two, you can coppice alternate trees every three years (meaning individual trees will be coppiced at intervals of six years). Most hazel poles will last two or three years so by the time you need to renew them, you can coppice the second tree which will now have six-year-old growth. To enable plants to grow under the coppiced hazel, you can remove the lower side branches to allow more light to the base of the hazel.

Willow and hazel are also lovely wood to whittle. During lockdown I bought myself an inexpensive knife and spent many a contemplative hour around the fire pit practising my knife skills by stripping bark or simply making a point on a stick before working up to spatula and spoon carving. You can use your practice sticks as kindling and the wood shavings make great tinder if, like me, you enjoy lighting your fire using a flint and steel.

Using willow to weave some keyhole beds and bed edges to prevent the plants from covering the paths

Gathering willow bark stripped from some poles. The bark is coiled up and dried. When I am ready to weave with it, I will soak it and uncoil it.

My favorite willows for weaving

These coppicing willows can either be planted individually with a spread of around 1.5m or can be planted in blocks or rows with a spacing of 40cm. Planting them closer together means they produce longer, straighter rods. If planted individually, rods will tend to be curved as the rods grow outwards then upwards.

Salix daphnoides **'Continental Purple'**

This willow produces a variety of sizes of rods so you have a source of both larger structural rods and finer ones for basketry from one plant. It can get large if unpruned but if coppiced for rods it will be around 1.5-2m in height.

Salix purpurea **'Dicky Meadows'**

This variety produces straight, fine rods up to 1.8m long, perfect for basket making. The bark dries to a beautiful pale grey/green.

Salix alba **'Vitellina'**

The colour of these rods is a vibrant yellow/orange growing up to 2m each year. They are long and straight with little branching, making them ideal for basketry.

Salix alba fragilis **'Flanders Red'**

The rods, growing up to 3m, are green in summer, turning to red in winter and drying to orange. It has a waxy skin which makes it a pleasure to weave with. It is a beautiful willow to grow as an ornamental in the garden.

My go-to willow for structures is *Salix viminalis*. Each year, rods will grow to 2m or more. The rods are straight and strong, much thicker than basketry willow, and perfect for weaving living willow structures. The smaller rods can be used for large baskets. I also grow a hybrid fast-growing variety of *viminalis* which grows rods up to 4m long each year. I grow this to turn into wood chip as a mulch for my garden but I have also used the strong rods for plant supports and two-year-old rods for firewood.

Other plants you can grow for weaving

Bindweed (*Convovulus arvensis*)

It's always good to have a use for some of the most pernicious weeds that cause problems in the garden. Bindweed can be used for non-structural weaving. I'm sure someone with a bindweed problem will be more than happy for you to clear some from their garden. If you leave cut stems to wilt for 24 hours, the leaves rub off without damaging the stem.

Blackberry 'Thornfree' (*Rubus fruticosus*)

The thorns on any bramble can be removed by rubbing up and down the stem while wearing a thick pair of gloves but growing a thornless variety removes this processing step. It can be used fresh in foraged and rustic style baskets to weave but is not great for the structural parts.

A beautiful foraging basket woven with a mix of fibres, not my basket but photographed at a permaculture festival

Dogwood (*Cornus alba*)

Cultivars have colourful straight stems if coppiced each year. They are not as flexible as willow but are still very useful for weaving. Ideally cut and leave to dry before using. Rehydrate just before weaving by soaking in water, this reduces shrinkage. *Cornus alba* 'Kesselringii' has beautiful blackish purple stems. *C.* 'Sibirica' stems are vibrant red. *Cornus sanguinea* 'Midwinter Fire' has very striking colouring with the tips starting as a fiery orange and gradually fading to yellow at the base. This variety is more branching so not as good for fine weaving, such as baskets and bed edges, but look beautiful used for plant supports.

Holly (*Ilex* sp.)

Long, thin growth is flexible enough to be used for weaving. Perhaps not fine enough for basketry but certainly for larger obelisks and plant supports.

Honeysuckle (*Lonicera periclymenum*)

Use the flexible younger growth for weaving; harvest in the autumn when it is the most flexible. Remove the leaves by running a gloved hand along the stem. Coil up the stems and boil in a pan of water for a few hours. Remove the bark by scraping it off whilst the stems are still hot. The process of boiling also strengthens the stems.

Lime (*Tilia* sp.)

You will often see mature lime trees in public parks and gardens which have lots of branches and leaves at the base of the tree. These are called suckers and are usually cut back each year. The suckers can be harvested when the leaves have dropped and are very flexible and fine, perfect for a rustic basket.

Winter-flowering jasmine (*Jasminum nudiflorum*)

Flowering in winter/early spring it provides valuable fodder for pollinating insects early in the year.

Wisteria sp.

You can harvest very long stems of new growth from wisteria in the dormant season which need cutting back anyway to encourage them to flower.

A woven willow obelisk made from a combination of willows using *Salix viminalis* for the uprights

Cordage, twine and infill weaving

I like to provide for all my gardening needs from the plants around me, including string. When I need to tie back some unruly peas, I simply cut a leaf from a New Zealand flax (*Phormium tenax*), peel off a thin strip of the leaf and use that directly as my string. Minimum faff or processing. It is a surprisingly strong fibre with the added bonus that it can be composted along with the dead stems at the end of the year without adding any micro-plastic fibres to the soil. Jute string can also be composted but has a lot of embodied energy in the form of the growing, harvesting, processing, packaging and transport. Fibres grown in your own garden using organic techniques are the most sustainable option.

If you are wanting something more robust or long-lasting you can make your own cordage. It is an enjoyable but time consuming process so I wouldn't use handmade cordage for tying in my peas but I may use it to tie up a bundle of canes, as a loop to hang a chopping board, to tie a label to a jar or to create some homemade bunting.

The process is relatively simple. It is usually best to dry the leaves if you pick them fresh, then rehydrate when you want to make cord as fresh leaves and stems can shrink as they dry, causing your tightly twisted cord to separate and become loose. Simply harvest your chosen fibre, lay it out in a thin layer to dry, then tie into a bundle at the cut end and hang upside down to finish drying and to store. When you are ready to make twine, rehydrate in water for a few hours to a few days, each plant varies. The bath can be handy as you can lay long leaves or branches without them snapping, then leave wrapped in a wet towel overnight to ensure even rehydration. You can then tear the leaves into strips, the finer the strips, the finer the cordage will be.

Cordage process

Take a piece of your fibre and make a twist, not in the middle but with one end longer than the other, hold the

Twine is made by twisting pieces of fibre together until it pulls itself together

Finished twine made from dried then rehydrated *Iris sibirica* leaves

fibre between your fingers and twist until a loop begins to form. Let this loop come together. Rolling one piece of fibre between your fingers, twist it away from yourself then pass it behind the other length. Take the front length and twist again away from yourself and then pass this behind the other length. Continue this process until one of the lengths gets near to the end. Keep the twists tight. If you are doing it right, the cord will twist together to form a neat cord. You can then simply add a fresh piece of fibre into the 'V', ensuring you have at least a few centimetres left of the original length, and twist this new length together with the piece you will be replacing, no need for knots. This is also why you start with differing lengths at the beginning, to ensure you don't have the joins of both pieces at the same point in the cord, as this will make the join weak and lumpy. It can take practice. It is challenging to explain this process in writing so I recommend finding an online tutorial or someone who can show you. I taught a group of friends one evening over a cup of tea and piece of cake and we found it quite addictive and hard to stop once started.

An alternative method is simply to plait the strips of fibres, adding new pieces in as the length runs out, just as with the twisting method.

The flowers of daylily are beautiful and edible but it is the leaves that can be used to make cordage

Plants for cordage

New Zealand flax (*Phormium tenax*)

There are many different cultivars of various colours and sizes. I like to use 'Jester' and 'Platts Black' as they break up the monotony of green foliage in the garden. They are cultivated as a source of fibre for traditional Maori rope making, textiles and basketry. You can peel strips off and use straight away. To process for making rope, cord and textile fibres, scrape the leaves to expose and extract the fibres. They are evergreen so a great source of string year round.

Siberian iris (*Iris sibirica*)

The flowers are one of my favourites and I use them a lot in my designs, so I was delighted to learn the leaves can be used for making cordage. Leaves are best harvested in the autumn as the fibres are strongest then. Dry in thin layers then tie in bundles and hang them from the base of the leaves. *Iris douglasii* is another species with suitable leaves. It is evergreen which makes it valuable as it can be harvested through the winter.

Daylily (*Hemerocallis* sp.)

It's not enough that every part of this plant is edible, its leaves can also be used for making cordage.

Montbretia (*Crocosmia* sp.)

Some cultivars have better leaves than others. I am still experimenting. 'Emberglow' is a huge and beautiful variety but the leaves can be a bit stiff and rigid. The montbretia I have spent decades trying to eradicate from clients' gardens has more pliable but shorter leaves. I need to experiment a bit more before I can decide which is the ideal one for twining.

Natural dye plants

There are a huge number of plants that can be used to create eco-friendly natural dyes and pigments for use with textiles, yarn, paints, inks and pastels. Natural fabric dying can get quite technical and it is a whole other book's worth of information to explain mordants, altering colours by adjusting pH and more. Here I will give details of some of the most popular plants and some easy ways they can be used creatively. I have painted from an early age but over the years have limited my materials as I became unhappy with the pollution and waste associated with the paints I was using. I do still buy watercolour paints but since discovering it is possible to make your own, I have been researching and collecting suitable plants to grow in the garden to create my own pigments.

Natural pigments give very variable results; this is one of the most exciting things about creating your own dyes from plants, you never know exactly what you will end up with. Healthy plants that have put on lush growth could produce a different shade to the same variety of plant that has struggled along with a lack of water and nutrients. If you don't have much room for your dye garden, try to choose three plants to cover the primary colours of red, blue and yellow so you can mix your own new colours from the three basics. There are plenty of vegetable scraps you can use straight from the kitchen to produce dyes, such as onion skins, spinach, beetroot and red cabbage. It may be a good idea to practise with these before committing to planting a whole dye garden to see if you enjoy the process. You may well find you already have a few of the listed plants in your garden and can give it a try straight away.

Jars of dried flowers can be used for dying fabric any time of year; summer is quite a busy time so it is nice to dry craft materials to use in the winter when you may want to spend more time indoors

List of dye plants

Dyer's chamomile (*Cota tinctoria*)

A yellow dye can be obtained from the flowers. It is happy in full sun in poor or moderately fertile, well-drained, dry soil and prefers slightly alkaline to neutral soil. Its height and spread are 30-60cm. It produces an abundance of bright yellow flowers from June until September.

Weld (*Reseda luteola*)

This produces a yellow dye from the leaves, stem and flowers. It prefers full sun on well-drained soil and is drought tolerant once established. Weld thrives in a variety of soil types, but it prefers alkaline soils although I have grown it successfully on acid soil. Height 1-1.5m, spread 40-60cm. Weld flowers from June to October.

Madder (*Rubia tinctorum*)

The roots of madder produce a red dye. The plant is quite sprawling so make sure it isn't next to anything too small that would be easily smothered. Madder prefers full sun to partial shade and well-drained, slightly alkaline soil. It may need watering in very dry conditions. Height 0.9-1.2m, spread 0.75-1m. Roots should be harvested in winter when the plant is dormant.

Dyer's coreopsis (*Coreopsis tinctoria*)

The flowers produce a yellow dye. It is a very attractive plant for the dye garden. It prefers full sun, well-drained

Dyer's chamomile has beautiful yellow flowers which make a yellow dye soil and is drought tolerant once established. It prefers slightly acidic to neutral soil. Height 40-90cm, spread 30-60cm. Flowers are available to harvest from June to September.

Woad (*Isatis tinctoria*)

A blue dye can be obtained from the leaves although it can be challenging to extract. Woad grows happily in full sun or part shade. It prefers a well-drained soil, preferably slightly alkaline to neutral and not too fertile. It is a biennial so flowers in its second year then dies. Its foliage grows to around 30-40cm height and spread in its first year. The flowers reach a height of 0.6-1.2m with a spread of 0.6-1m. It flowers in mid to late summer.

Goldenrod (*Solidago* sp.)

The flowers are used to make a bright yellow dye. They prefer full sun and well-drained soil but can tolerate quite sandy poor soil and I have seen them growing happily in quite a bit of shade.

The most common variety is *Solidago canadensis* which can be invasive and quite a large plant at a height of around 0.75-1.5m but any goldenrod will work. The European native goldenrod, *Solidago virgaurea*, also grows to over 1m. More modern, compact varieties are now available: 'Golden Fleece' with a height and spread of 60cm and 40cm and 'Fireworks' with a height and spread of 90cm. Goldenrod flowers in late summer into autumn.

Other dye plants

- Red/Pink – Goat willow (*Salix caprea*), beetroot (*Beta vulgaris*), dock roots (*Rumex obtusifolius*), rhubarb roots (*Rheum* sp.)
- Orange – Brown onion skins (*Allium cepa*), marigolds (*Tagetes* sp.)
- Yellow – Pot marigold (*Calendula officinalis*), dyer's greenweed (*Genista tinctoria*)
- Green – Foxglove (*Digitalis purpurea*), spinach (*Spinacia oleracea*), cow parsley (*Anthriscus sylvestris*)
- Blue – Japanese indigo (*Persicaria tinctoria*), cornflower (*Centaurea cyanus*)
- Purple – Elderberries (*Sambucus nigra*), blackthorn berries (*Prunus spinosa*)
- Brown – Walnut hulls (*Juglans regia*), tea (*Camellia sinensis*), oak galls (*Quercus* sp.)

Filtering the dye liquid to extract the blue pigment from woad

Goldenrod has a beautiful yellow flower that is great for pollinators

Craft garden

I have taken the original plan for the craft garden at Esholt Hall and updated it with plants I have been researching and trying out since the first design was created in 2022. My first passion before I moved into horticulture was sculpture. I love manipulating natural materials into useful and decorative items. At Esholt we wove bird houses, plant supports, bed edges and archways. We used willow and hazel rods to create plant labels, art easels and to make charcoal. Nettle, dandelion and New Zealand flax were used to make cordage. Dyer's chamomile, weld and madder were used to make pigments for dyeing fabrics and making natural watercolour paints. Our gardens can offer so much in the way of material for crafting.

The vision for the craft garden

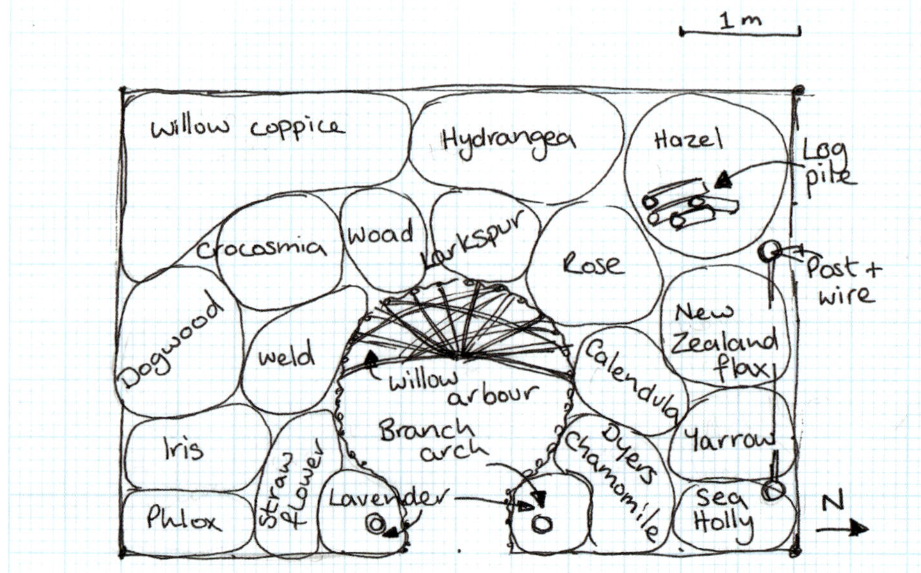

The planting plan for the craft garden

A woven willow arbour is at the centre of the design for the craft garden

Dahlias make fantastic and colourful cut flowers. They also have edible petals.

Plant list for craft garden

Weaving and cordage

Dogwood 'Sibirica' (*Cornus alba*)
Hazel (*Corylus avellana*)
Iris sibirica 'Butter and Sugar'
Japanese honeysuckle (*Lonicera japonica*)
Montbretia 'Red King' (*Crocosmia* x *crocosmiiflora*)
Nettle (*Urtica dioica*)
New Zealand flax 'Maori Queen' (*Phormium tenax*)
Willow 'Flanders Red' (*Salix alba fragilis*)

Dye plants

Calendula officinalis
Dyer's chamomile (*Cota tinctoria*)
Madder (*Rubia tinctorum*)
Weld (*Reseda luteola*)
Woad (*Isatis tinctoria*)

Cut flowers for drying

Achillea 'Fanal' (*Achillea millefolium*)
Giant sea holly 'Silver Ghost' (*Eryngium giganteum*)
Hydrangea 'Endless Summer' (*Hydrangea macrophylla*)
Larkspur 'Limelight Light Pink' (*Delphinium consolida*)
Lavender (*Lavandula angustifolis, L. stoechas*)
Phlox 'Windsor' (*Phlox paniculata*)
Rose 'Jacqueline du Pré' (*Rosa* sp.)
Strawflower 'Granvia Pink' (*Xerochrysum bracteatum*)

Designing Esholt Hall Gardens

Using my collages as inspiration as I play with ideas for the site

Designing a garden is about so much more than deciding the shape of your patio or choosing a colour palette.

Every time I start a new design I begin with a conversation with the client. Each person's wants and needs are as diverse as the sites they garden in. Esholt Hall Gardens has been a complex design in this respect as the main design brief came from Yorkshire Water who wanted to include a wellbeing garden for staff as this is their training academy site. It also needed to fulfil the requirements of Sponge Tree, the organisation tasked with the garden project who wanted to develop it as a community garden and teaching space. I was overjoyed to get the job of designing and helping to create the permaculture garden at Esholt Hall, set within a walled garden and surrounded by mature woodland. A truly beautiful place to create something special.

A preliminary design had already been proposed including raised beds, a herb area and a rectangular forest garden. Ideally at this point you would bring all the community together to help co-design the space. Unfortunately due to health and safety issues we couldn't have volunteers on site so it was up to Paula (project manager), Chris and myself to imagine what would be needed. Luckily we had many years of community gardening experience to draw from.

Raised beds are a great way to make growing spaces more accessible to those in wheelchairs or those with mobility issues. We designed these to have plenty of space for manoeuvring. Local students from Bradford College came to practise their carpentry skills and did a brilliant job of constructing the beds, gaining real life experience of working on a site, adding to the many yields from this project. The beds were filled with a mix of topsoil from the garden and compost made by Plate to Plate, a small local business taking domestic and business food waste and turning it into quality compost. It has been important throughout the project that materials are sourced locally and ethically and this is just as vital a part of the design process as the planting plans or path layout.

The snaking path I designed for the apothecary garden

The walled garden had been very neglected and was mostly weeds, turf and paving

Apothecary garden

Paula and I both have an interest in the healing properties of herbs so rather than simply including culinary herbs I designed an apothecary garden. It was such a rich learning experience designing this part of the garden as I have very little experience of using herbs for healing but over the years (once you hit 40, it feels like your body starts falling to bits) I have looked to natural remedies for inflammation issues and to boost my immune system. Plants such as evening primrose (*Oenothera biennis*), mullein (*Verbascum thapsus*) and ribwort plantain (*Plantago lanceolata*) had self-seeded around the formal garden and were relocated to the apothecary beds. Plantain has now become my most used garden plant for first aid. I learnt how to make a spit poultice by chewing the leaves gently to release the juices before putting them on bites, stings and rashes. I wanted to design with plants that are easy to process and useful for a variety of ailments so I included many which can simply be picked and added to hot water to make herbal tea. These include marshmallow (*Althaea officinalis*),

Weaving the snaking bed edges using willow from Esholt's willow coppice which we were restoring

lemon balm (*Melissa officinalis*), lavender (*Lavandula angustifolia* formerly *L. officinalis*) and several types of mint. I learnt the word *officinalis* in a plant name refers to its use as a medicine in the past, derived from the Latin word 'opificina' meaning herb store or pharmacy.

The site is rich in resources with a willow coppice, self-seeded plants, rock piles, huge mountains of woodchip and planked wood from onsite tree felling. Much of the aesthetic of the garden comes from using these resources in preference to buying anything in. The same design layout in a different location would have looked very different as many ideas were born from wandering around the site to see what I could use. We really did use and value these renewable resources. We wove curving path edges from willow and included keyhole beds. I like to use keyhole beds in designs as they allow easy access to the beds for harvesting and weeding whilst minimising paths. A pond is sited at the shadier end of the herb garden to help keep it cool in summer. It was wonderful to observe how quickly life moved into the pond. Less than 12 months on and Paula caught a glimpse of a newt.

A keyhole bed in the apothecary garden with yarrow, olive herb, evening primrose, lavender mint and oregano

Plants were foraged from around the garden and grown from seed, cuttings and divisions

The pond in the corner of the apothecary garden added hugely important habitat for wildlife

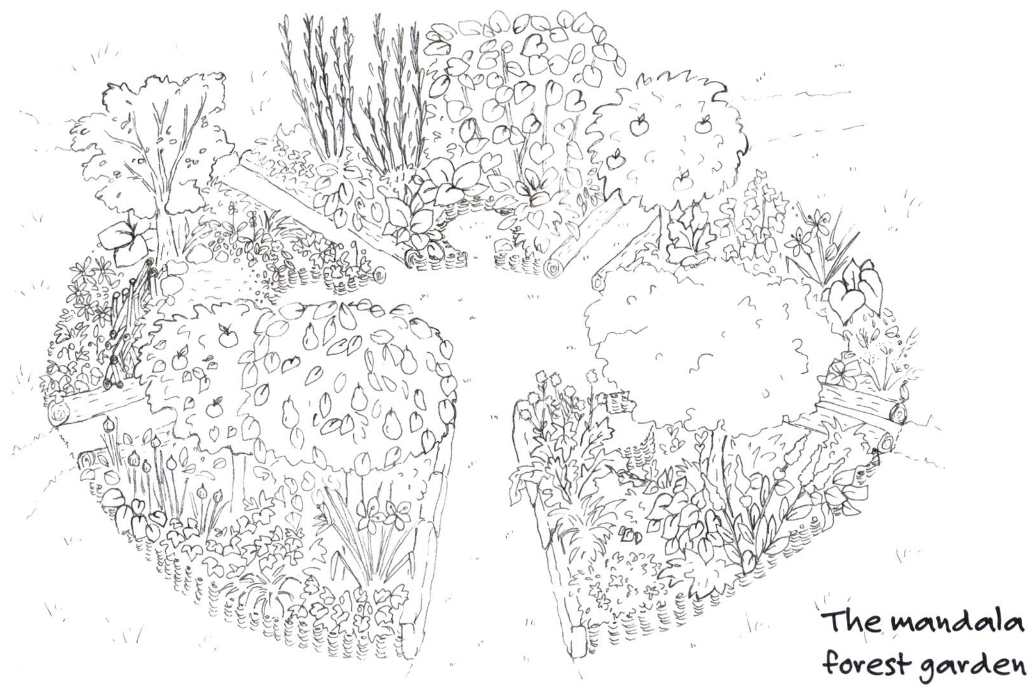

The mandala forest garden

Mandala forest garden

The feature I found the most rewarding to design is the mandala forest garden. The original plan was for a rectangular garden but standing in a walled garden next to raised beds and straight edged paths I felt it needed something softer. I started by deciding the teaching/wellbeing space should be in the centre of the garden. This would create a feeling of being immersed in nature and give privacy. I would then wrap the forest garden around this space, like a big forest garden hug. At the ideas phase, I had begun to collect images and create collages. This unleashed my creativity, looking through books, magazines and online image libraries and sparking inspiration from all sorts of sources, from other gardens to sculptures and architecture. Spending time playing with images, scissors, pens and glue makes me slow down, giving time to process my ideas and come up with something that excites me, something new I couldn't have imagined without the collage process.

One image I was drawn to was a mandala, which fitted perfectly with the idea of a space for wellbeing. By splitting the garden into segments, I could give each section a theme, highlighting the many functions and uses of plants within a forest garden other than food. The sections include habitat and wildlife forage plants, medicinal plants, natural dye plants, fibre plants for weaving and cordage making and food plants. Within these segments, I chose plants to extend the season as much as possible, especially with the forage plants for pollinators. Crocus and muscari come up early in the year for those warm, late winter days when bees are venturing out. There are many plants flowering all spring and summer followed by geranium 'Rozanne' and rudbeckia 'Goldsturm', flowering right up until the first hard frosts of the year.

Over the years my depth of appreciation of the forest garden ecosystem has increased, resulting in designs with plentiful habitat features. After all, if we want to practice fair shares, it's important to remember that permaculture gardens are not just for us humans. Diversity is essential to provide shelter and food sources for as many species as possible. At Esholt Hall Gardens we were lucky to have a plentiful supply of both deciduous and coniferous wood to use for bed edges and log piles. A curving dead hedge stuffed with willow and apple prunings provides a central feature within one

The dead hedge is next to a pond so creatures have a source of water and shelter. These are in the centre of the bed for least disturbance from visitors.

The mandala garden is all planted. In five or ten year's time this garden will look completely different as the trees and shrubs mature. The planting will change as the amount of shade increases and the features also, as Paula and Chris and their volunteers create new habitat and try out new things.

Plants such as teasels are there for the wildlife

segment next to a small pond and a stone pile. We tried not to be too tidy as all sorts of creatures have now set up home in the garden. It fills me with joy to see the garden buzzing with life and feels to me like a brilliant measure of the success of the design.

The initial planting and build phase is now complete and I have had the immense pleasure of teaching a few forest gardening courses within it. As the trees and shrubs mature, the feeling of being wrapped up in the garden will increase. Until then, a simple woven fence with archways for climbers to grow on will give the garden some height. As a team, we coppiced the willow and wove the structure ourselves. It gives the garden such a sense of being grounded in the landscape to be constructed from the plants and materials surrounding it.

As with every design, each one informs the next. Many of the ideas I tried out at Esholt Hall will be incorporated into my new garden which is currently a blank canvas. I have much bigger plans for healing and medicinal plants than in my initial design for home. Plans are coming together for a community healing garden at Ecology Building Society, another garden I help manage, so more people have access to these important and powerful plants. If you are looking for ideas for

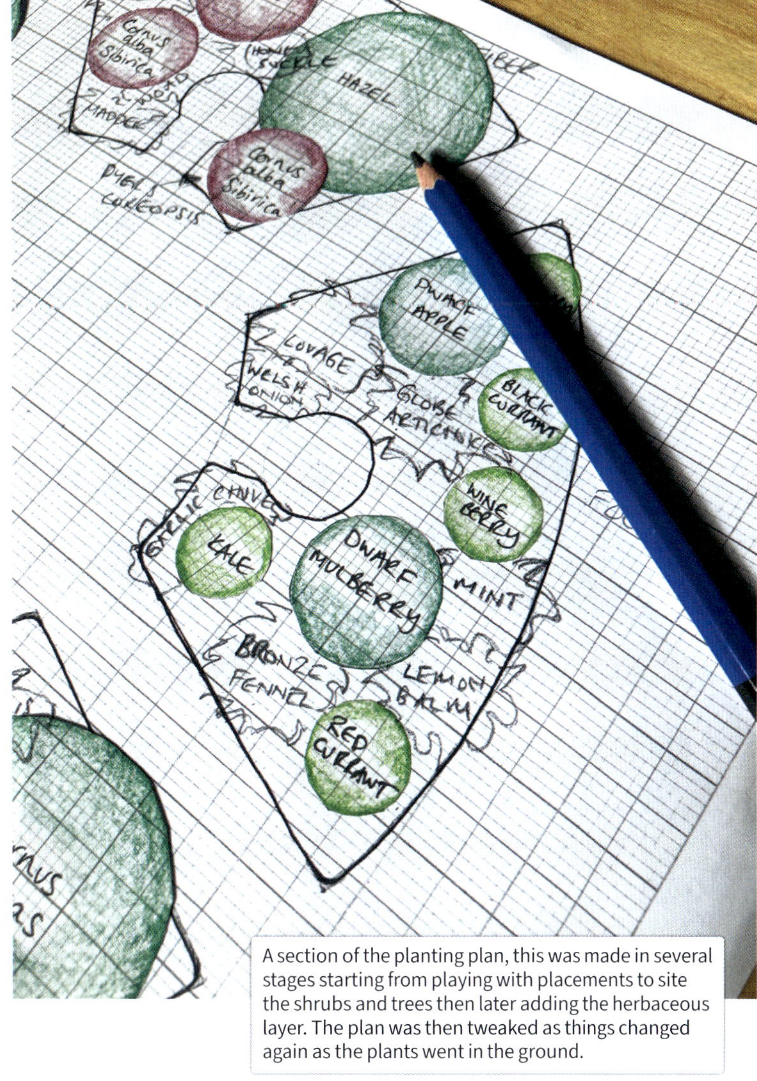

A section of the planting plan, this was made in several stages starting from playing with placements to site the shrubs and trees then later adding the herbaceous layer. The plan was then tweaked as things changed again as the plants went in the ground.

The mandala forest garden with a tent up, ready for teaching

your own garden, the best inspiration comes from visiting other gardens, there many permaculture projects globally open to the public. If you don't have the time, resources or ability to travel, then take a look in books, or watch online garden tours, there are so many amazing creative designers out there sharing what they do.

My best advice would be to start small and slow. Make an overall plan but break it up into individual areas or beds. As you complete one area, use what you have learnt to create a better design for the next area. Designs are never static. The garden at Esholt Hall will change over time. Some plants will fail, some will flourish, but that is what makes designing gardens so exciting.

Paula harvesting mallow flowers to use for making paint pigments

Bringing your Design to Life

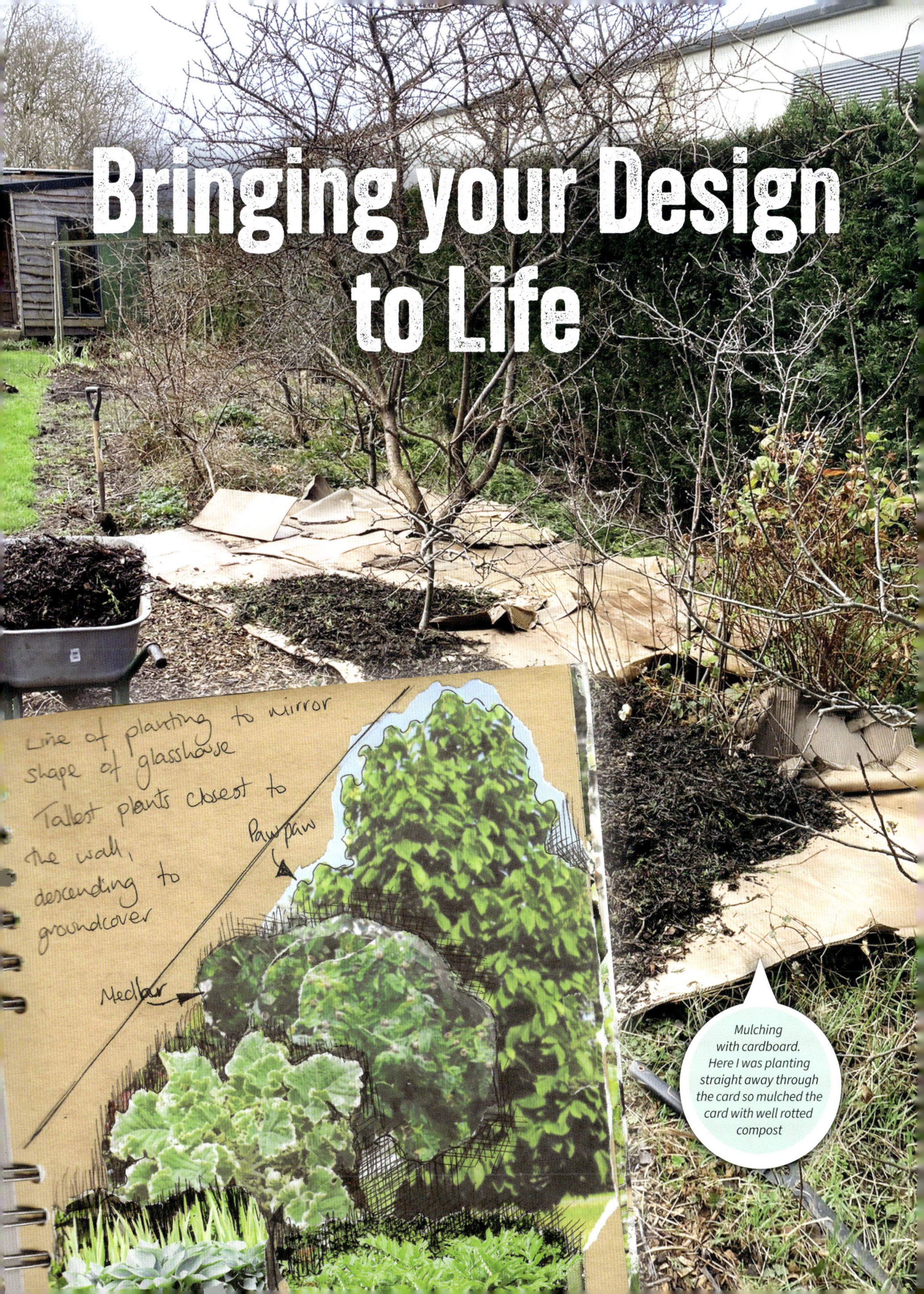

Mulching with cardboard. Here I was planting straight away through the card so mulched the card with well rotted compost

Preparing your site

You've planned and mapped out your dream garden, now it's finally time to bring it to life. But before the first plant goes in the ground, preparing your site is vital to the long-term success of any design.

As discussed in the chapter Getting to Know your Garden, the ideal is to plant according to your conditions. No-dig is also something to aspire to but if your ground is very compacted or has very stony soil full of rubble, it is reasonable to want to make some improvements before planting. It is a personal choice of weighing up how many inputs, with their environmental costs, you are comfortable to import against the benefits of increased yields you will gain over many years into the future.

In my current new garden, I am digging the top 15cm to relieve surface compaction then adding a thick mulch of composted bark and manure. This compaction would eventually be reduced by the action of roots growing in the soil and worm activity but by that time, the trees and shrubs will have had a bad start and I want to give them the best possible chance to make a healthy root system. After the initial improvement year, I will simply add a mulch each year in late winter and this organic matter will slowly improve the soil as it gets worked into the ground by worms and other burrowing creatures.

Mulch with cut grass to kill off the turf

If you do dig over your plot or import a deep layer of topsoil, spend some time shuffling over the whole surface once to tread it down. Don't worry, this won't be enough to compact it again. I have seen plant root balls sitting several centimeters above the soil level due to soil settling after planting. This can be fixed by replanting but you don't want to give yourself unnecessary work.

Recycled weed membrane kills off weeds and grass. We left it down for 12 months then peeled it back, planted, then mulched straight away.

We laid out the shape of the beds for the apothecary garden at Esholt Hall using rope to try out different shapes

Plants are laid on the bed, and moved around until I am happy with the whole design

Laying out your design

There are several ways to do this. A lot depends on the size of your plot and whether it is a blank canvas or you're planting into an existing mature garden. I like to gather all the plants together and lay my pots out in the space, making adjustments and moving them about until I am happy with how they all fit in. If you have a large design, you may want to mark out 1m squares so you can be more precise about following your to-scale plan. Mark these out using rope, hosepipe, string or even a thin line of sand. This way you can lay out and plant a small area at a time. If it is a very large area, you can give each square a reference number and write a list of all the plants needed for that square. It depends on how much of an organised and precise person you are; I prefer to freestyle it a bit more.

If you are planting into a mature garden, you can simply lay out plants in the spaces you have made. You can add canes with labels attached during spring, summer or autumn if you are going to be planting in the dormant season and it may not be clear later on, where the existing plants are once they have died down.

If you decided not to draw up a to-scale plan then simply lay out the pots and move them around until you are happy. This is how I do many of my designs at home, when I don't need to make plans for a client, but I have many years of experience. If you are new to designing your garden, you may want a plan to make sure you don't overbuy or underbuy plants and to make sure you are putting them in an appropriate place to meet their requirements.

I lay out the pots then throw the bulbs around them so that I plant everything at the same time

Planting

As you put the plants in the ground, make sure you push down on the soil you have pulled back around the plant. You want to avoid pockets of air and ensure the plant roots have made good contact with the soil. Watering your scheme straight after planting will help to wash soil around the roots. Add a mulch to help retain water and to add organic matter and nutrients to the soil. Ensure plants do not get water-stressed during their first year; it is also important to let them send their roots down into the ground in search of water, this will make them more resilient to drought in the future. Water well and not too often. Once a week should be enough in dry spells. If in doubt, get your hands into the soil and see how dry or moist it feels below the surface.

Maintenance

One of the main benefits of a perennial garden is the reduced work to maintain it. No need for sowing seed, pricking out, trying to avoid damping off, planting out and fighting off the slugs for every single crop. I have compiled this section to give an easy overview of the main tasks in your garden to carry out in each season.

Each garden will have different needs so just as with the plant portfolio, it is worth spending time checking the care requirements for each plant in your garden and adding it to a plan. That way you can easily follow the plan, safe in the knowledge you are doing everything at the right time and in the right order. This plan can develop over time as plants mature or die off or you amend your design. You may decide to add a pond after a few years so you can then add the appropriate pond maintenance task to each season.

When and how to prune is one of the most common questions I get asked. When I was learning, I bought a pruning book from a charity shop and learnt by doing, by jumping in with both feet and being brave. Now there is the assistance of YouTube and online searches to demonstrate how, so don't be afraid and give it a go. You are very, very unlikely to kill a shrub or tree by pruning it badly. At worst you will end up with an oddly shaped plant and lose a year's worth of fruit. As a minimum, remove the dead, diseased and dying branches and stems. I don't prune my fruit as the books advise, I mostly leave them to do their own thing and only intervene when I feel it is necessary.

Weeding should not be a huge task if you have added plenty of weed suppressing ground cover plants in your design and mulch each year. I often find it is the crop plants that I am digging up or cutting back as they get a bit too vigorous or start to swamp out their neighbour. A weed is defined as a plant in the wrong place so if you have a problem with a plant, before you put in the effort to remove it, first check that it doesn't have a use you didn't know about. You may discover you are lucky to have it.

Try not to be over tidy; that 'mess' is vital habitat or a food source for part of your garden's food web. Rather than cutting back and removing plant stems and leaves, simply chop them up and leave them to rot down in situ. This 'chop and drop' technique saves the time and energy of removing plant material to a compost heap then bringing it back again. It also helps to protect the soil over winter and prevents heavy winter rains from compacting the soil surface. If adding mulch, this can be done in winter or spring but ideally before the bulbs come up as this will make mulching a very fiddly job.

Irrigation should be unnecessary after the first establishment year. During drought conditions you may wish to water any plants that are looking water-stressed but if you do intervene, make sure you water enough for it to soak the ground. Wetting just the surface encourages more shallow surface roots which makes the plant even less able to manage future droughts. A good deep mulch should be all that is necessary if you have chosen the correct plants. If you are having to water often, you may consider replacing the plants that are suffering with something more drought tolerant.

Chop and drop stems go directly onto the ground and rot down in situ providing nutrients and organic matter to the soil

Maintenance Calendar

Brunnera 'Jack Frost' covered in spring blooms

Spring

Add compost or mulch to the surface of the soil to enrich soil, feed soil life and help retain soil moisture.

Sow annual seeds either in situ, in pots outdoors or in a cold frame, greenhouse or propagator.

Check for any invasive weeds or plants that may need removing or reducing.

Prune dead or diseased wood from trees and shrubs. Young stone fruit trees such as plum, cherry and apricots should be pruned in April to avoid infection by silverleaf, a fungal disease that can enter via pruning cuts.

Check irrigation and water-harvesting systems are still functioning.

Add new plants where there are any gaps. You can identify gaps as the plants start to spring into life.

Prune out old raspberry canes of autumn-fruiting raspberries.

Plant out tender annuals once risk of frost is over.

Make notes of observations.

Autumn is a busy time for harvesting and preserving before the long cold months of winter

Summer

Check on mulch to ensure soil is not drying out.

If watering is needed, water deeply but not frequently.

Monitor pest attacks; it can take a while for beneficial insects to turn up but any sprays, even neem oil and organic ones, are damaging to the good guys as well. If a plant is suffering, consider mechanical action, such as picking off or using a jet of water to dislodge pests.

Thin (remove some) fruit on trees where the weight of fruit may cause branches to snap. Carry out summer pruning on all top fruit (apple, pear, cherry, plum etc.) to remove dead, diseased or dying branches and to reduce the vigour and size of trees.

Established stone fruit including plums, cherries and apricots should be pruned in July to reduce the risk of infection from silverleaf, a fungal disease that can enter via pruning cuts.

Make liquid feed from nettles and comfrey for those vigorous plants who may need a boost of nutrients.

Keep an observation diary of any insects or other wildlife you see in the garden.

Apple mint and tansy mingle happily in a wild grassy area of the garden after escaping from a neglected herb spiral

Autumn

Harvest seeds for propagation and to give to friends, neighbours and to offer at seed swaps.

Chop and drop dead plants if you can't bear to let them stand over winter. Don't chop these pieces too small as they are an important habitat for overwintering insects. You could create a bug snug which is an organised pile of dead stems and leaves to provide overwintering places for wildlife.

You can prune in autumn but plant growth is slowing down and wounds can be slow to heal. I prefer to prune in spring, so long as you are not removing the branches that will be producing flowers that year. If you need to prune in autumn, try to do it in early autumn while the plant is still actively growing and more likely to heal quickly.

Plant spring-flowering bulbs from autumn and into winter.

Winter is the perfect time to create new infrastructure, such as this archway made from willow and hazel poles and willow weavers. I designed these to mimic the stone carvings at Esholt Hall.

Winter

This is the time of year for infrastructure maintenance on paths, fences and sheds etc. Make repairs and repaint, rewax or revarnish where necessary.

Repair and sharpen tools, don't forget to oil wooden handles with linseed oil. Look out for repair cafes if you want to learn these valuable skills and to borrow the appropriate tools.

January is a good month for coppicing willow, hazel and other coppice trees and shrubs.

Apples and pears are traditionally pruned in winter as you can see their structure. New thinking is that too much winter pruning can actually cause an increase in leafy, branching growth, reducing air circulation and the light levels in the centre of the tree. I do very little winter pruning unless I am growing trained fruit or I am trying to keep a tree smaller than it wants to be.

Reflect on your observations from the year (this is why keeping a diary is so helpful). What has gone well, what has not? What changes would you like to make for next year? How would you like to do things differently? Make a plan for the coming year. This may simply be a list of tasks or a whole new design with tweaked planting plans and propagation list.

Take time for reading and research. Look back through your observation notes from the year and plan any changes you want to make for the next growing season.

Make a plant wishlist and order now before nurseries sell out.

Lift and divide plants you want to propagate and replant or pot up. Now is also the time for taking hardwood cuttings.

Clean out nesting boxes where necessary.

Plant spring bulbs if not done already.

Start your Polyculture Adventure Today

Why wait?

I often have conversations with people about the yearning to find an acre of land to be able to grow a food forest or a large productive garden, or whether they can wait until they fully understand garden design and how to create the 'perfect' plant combinations. My answer is always the same, stop waiting and start where you are.

I loved this tiny community garden in just a few raised beds in Poole

These tiny alpine strawberries can be grown in the smallest of spaces, even a window box

Some of the solutions covered in this book are inventive and fun, such as growing pumpkins upwards along washing lines and building pallet planters to grow salads vertically, safe from slugs and with plenty of light. Try to add an element of fun into your own design process, it will make the end design much more creative and mean you actually finish and implement it. I hope techniques described in this book have turned planting design from a daunting task into a fun process.

With careful design and observation, you would be surprised how much you can supplement your diet from even a small garden. Try not to overwhelm yourself with the goal of full self-sufficiency, you will find that you can increase yields each year as your garden matures and you develop a palate that enjoys more perennial greens. The use of the word 'forest' is pretty unhelpful when talking about smaller gardens but I hope I have shown that you absolutely can grow a multilayered food garden in a space as small as a raised bed.

You can meet so many of your needs from your garden whilst sharing the space with other creatures by creating log piles, small ponds and adding plants for pollinators. My goal is to be able to make a basket using only materials from my own garden. I would like to make all my own watercolour paints from natural pigments grown in my garden. What are your goals? Have they changed now that you have explored the many ideas in this book?

When growing a forest garden next to your home, its beauty becomes an important aspect too. Joy is such an underrated yield from a permaculture garden whether it's the satisfaction of harvesting your first crop or soaking up the beautiful views as you come and go. By making your garden beautiful as well as useful, you will inspire others to do the same. Soon you may find other permaculture gardens full of edible and useful plants popping up around your neighbourhood.

There is often a reluctance to start a garden when in rented or short-term accommodation. There are so many yields we get from gardening other than the produce we can harvest. The therapeutic benefits of gardening are now well known, having your hands in the soil can change the chemicals being released in your brain, reducing anxiety and giving a serotonin boost.

You don't need to have huge harvests to get a lot of pleasure from your permaculture garden

A permaculture garden can be beautiful as well as productive as this border at Ecology Building Society proves. Bistort, hawthorn, daylily, Babington's leeks and apple are just a few of the edible plants in this bed.

Spending more time outdoors, whether actively gardening or simply observing how your garden is growing, can also improve your mental and physical health.

The permaculture ethics bring the wisdom that we are not just gardening for ourselves. Future care is about living in a way that will benefit future generations. The fruit tree you plant now in your garden may not give you fruit if you move home, but it will be a wonderful source of food for those who come next. It will also provide a perennial food source for bees and other pollinators who will search it out each spring.

I talk a lot about the importance of observing and interacting with your garden to learn how things grow, how to tweak your planting each year or adapt your maintenance plan depending on how the plants are interacting and developing. This learning is just as valuable as the food you pick from the garden and much can be learnt from even a very small garden; if and when you do find a more permanent growing space (if you don't have one already) you can bring all that rich learning with you. You will be able to produce a better design when equipped with some knowledge you wouldn't have had otherwise.

Embrace experimentation. Your planting plan is just the start of your polyculture escapades. Perennial planting is more permanent but can still be added to, changed around and played with. Adding in annuals can be fun as these can change each year. One year you may grow beans in a gap, the next year it may be sunflowers and the year after, courgette. Or you may enjoy being totally hands off and letting nature take the lead. This in itself is an experiment, seeing how plants interact if you leave them alone.

So why wait, start your polyculture garden adventures today. You can transition your existing garden by swapping a few plants at a time or clear an area and start from scratch. Build a raised bed or source a preloved large container and see how many of the seven layers you can achieve. You don't need to wait for the perfect time or until you have all the skills. Why not start where you are? The experimenting and learning can start today.

Plant Index

Position: Full Sun FS, Part Shade PS, Deep Shade DS
Remember the size is without pruning, things can be kept smaller with coppicing, pollarding and pruning

Plant name	**Height**	**Spread**	**Sun/Shade**
Trees			
Alder (*Alnus glutinosa* and *A. cordata*)	12m+	4-8m	FS/PS
Angelica tree (*Aralia elata*)	8-10m	8m+	PS
Apple 'Red Devil' (*Malus domestica*)	3-6m	3-6m	FS/PS
Beech (*Fagus sylvatica*)	30m+	8m+	FS/PS
Birch (*Betula pendula*)	25m+	12m+	FS/PS
Black locust (*Robinia pseudoacacia*)	25m+	8m+	FS
Cherry 'Morello' (*Prunus cerasus*)	2-4m	2-4m	FS/PS/DS
Chinese cedar (*Toona sinensis*)	20m	8m	FS
Chinese dogwood (*Cornus kousa*)	10m	6m	FS/PS
Chinese pepper tree (*Zanthoxylum simulans*)	4m	6m	FS/PS/DS
Cider gum (*Eucalyptus gunnii*)	30m	6m	FS
Crab apple (*Malus sylvestris*)	10m	4m	FS/PS
Hawthorn (*Crataegus monogyna*)	6m	6m	FS/PS
Hawthorn 'Arnold' (*C. arnoldiana*)	4-8m	4-8m	FS/PS
Judas tree (*Cercis siliquastrum*)	12m	10m	FS/PS
Lime (*Tilia* sp.)	30m	12m	FS/PS
Medlar 'Nottingham' (*Mespilus germanica*)	6m	6m	FS/PS
Pear 'Beth' (*Pyrus communis*)	2.5-8m	2-6m	FS/PS
Plum 'Czar' (*Prunus domestica*)	2.5-4m	2.5-4m	FS/PS
Plum 'Jubilee' (*Prunus domestica*)	2.5-4m	2.5-4m	FS/PS
Red mulberry (*Morus rubra*)	8-12m	4-8m	FS
Service berry (*Amelanchier canadensis*)	6m	3m	FS/PS
Snow gum (*Eucalyptus pauciflora* subsp. *Niphophila*)	6m	3.5m	FS
White willow (*Salix alba*)	25m	10m	FS

Plant name	Height	Spread	Sun/Shade
Shrubs			
Alder buckthorn (*Frangula alnus*)	4-8m	2.5-4m	FS/PS
Autumn olive (*Elaeagnus umbellata*)	5m	5m	FS/PS
Bamboo (*Fargesia* sp.)	2.5-4m	1-1.5m	FS/PS
Blackberry 'Thornfree' (*Rubus fruticosus*)	1.5-2.5m	1.5	FS/PS
Blackcurrant 'Ben Hope', 'Ben Sarek', Ebony' (*Ribes nigrum*)	1.5m	1m	FS/PS
Dogwood 'Sibirica' (*Cornus alba*)	2-4m	2-4m	FS/PS
Elder 'Black Lace' (*Sambucus nigra*)	6m	6m	FS/PS/DS
False indigo (*Amorpha fruticosa*)	2.5-4m	2.5-4m	FS/PS
Fig 'Brown Turkey' (*Ficus carica*)	2.5-4m	2.5-4m	FS
Fig 'Brunswick' (*Ficus caria*)	2.5-4m	2.5-4m	FS
Golden bamboo (*Phyllostachys aurea*)	2.5-3.5m	2-3m	FS/PS
Gooseberry 'Hinnomaki Green' (*Ribes uva-crispa*)	1.5m	1m	FS/PS
Gooseberry 'Hinnonmaki Red' (*Ribes uva-crispa*)	1.5m	1m	FS/PS
Gooseberry 'Invicta' (*Ribes uvacrispa*)	1.5m	1.5m	FS/PS
Hebe 'Midsummer Beauty' (*Veronica* sp.)	1.5-2.5m	1-1.5m	FS/PS
Hydrangea 'Endless Summer' (*Hydrangea macrophylla*)	1-1.5m	1-1.5m	PS
Japanese rose (*Rosa rugosa*)	1-1.5m	1-1.5m	FS/PS
Japanese quince (*Chaenomeles japonica*)	0.5-1m	1.5-2.5m	FS/PS
Kale 'Daubentons' (*Brassica oleracea ramosa*)	1.2m	1.2-1.5m	FS/PS
Kale 'Daubentons Panache' (*Brassica oleracea ramosa*)	1m	1.5m	FS/PS
Kale 'Taunton Deane'	1.5m	1.5m	FS/PS
Lavender 'Hidcote' (*Lavandula angustifolia*)	0.5m	0.5-1m	FS
New Zealand flax 'Maori Queen' (*Phormium tenax*)	2.5-4m	1.5-2.5m	FS/PS
Oleaster (*Elaeagnus angustifolia*, *E. umbellata*)	5m	5m	FS
Orange bladder senna (*Colutea* x *media*)	2.5-4m	2.5-4m	FS
Oregon grape 'Charity' (*Mahonia* x *media*)	2.5-4m	2.5-4m	FS/PS
Oregon grape 'Winter Sun' (*Mahonia* x *media*)	2.5-4m	1.5-2.5m	FS/PS/DS
Oregon grape (*Mahonia aquifolium*)	0.5-1m	1-1.5m	PS/DS

Plant name	Height	Spread	Sun/Shade
Perennial Kale 'Taunton Deane' (*Brassica* Acephala group)	2m	2m	FS/PS
Pink currant (*Ribes rubrum*)	1.2m	1.2m	FS/PS
Raspberry 'Malling Jewel' (*Rubus idaeus*)	1.5m	0.5m	PS/DS
Raspberry 'Autumn Treasure' (*Rubus idaeus*)	1m	1m	FS/PS
Raspberry 'Ruby Beauty' (*Rubus idaeus*)	2m	0.5m	FS
Redcurrant 'Rovada' (*Ribes rubrum*)	1-1.5m	1-1.5m	FS/PS
Rose, Apothecary's (*Rosa gallica* var. *officinalis*)	1m	1m	FS
Rose damascena	1.5-2m	1.5-2m	FS/PS
Rose 'Geranium' (*Rosa moyesii*)	2.5-4m	2.5-4m	FS/PS
Rose 'Jaqueline du Pre' (*Rosa* sp.)	1.2m	1m	FS
Rose 'Katharina Zeimet' (*Rosa sp.*)	60cm	90cm	FS
Rose, Moyes (*Rosa moyesii*)	2.5-4m	2.5-4m	FS
Rose, Dog (*Rosa canina*)	2.5-4m	1.5-2.5m	FS
Rosemary (*Salvia rosmarinus*)	1.5-2.5m	1.5-2.5m	FS
Sage 'Tricolor', 'Purpurascens Variegata', (*Salvia officinalis*)	0.5-1m	0.5-1m	FS
Saltbush (*Atriplex halimus*)	2m	3m	FS
Scotch broom (*Cytisus scoparius*)	2.5	1-1.5m	FS/PS
Sea buckthorn (*Hippophae rhamnoides*)	6m	3m	FS
Siberian pea tree (*Caragana arborescens*)	6m	4m	FS/PS
Silverberry (*Elaeagnus commutata*)	2-4m	1.5-2m	FS
Spanish broom (*Spartium junceum*)	3.5m	3m	FS
Stransvaesia (*Photinia davidiana*)	6m	4m	FS/PS
Trailing rosemary (*Salvia rosmarinus* Prostrata group)	0.5m	1m	FS
Wineberry (*Rubus phoenicolasius*)	3m	1m	FS/PS
Winter-flowering honeysuckle (*Lonicera fragrantissima*)	2m	2m	FS/PS
Winter-flowering jasmine (*Jasminum nudiflorum*)	1.5-2.5m	1.5-2.5m	FS/PS
Witch hazel (*Hamamelis virginiana*)	4-8m	2.5-4m	FS/PS

Plant name	Height	Spread	Sun/Shade
Herbaceous perennials			
Achillea 'Moonshine'	0.75m	0.5m	FS
Achillea 'Fanal'	0.75m	0.5m	FS
Achillea millefolium 'Summer Pastels'	0.3-0.6m	0.5m	FS
Allium moly (*Allium* sp.)	0.3m	0.1m	FS
Apple mint (*Mentha suaveolens*)	1m	0.8m	FS/PS
Arnica (*Arnica montana*)	0.1-0.5m	0.1-0.5m	FS
Aster 'Monch' (*Aster* x *frikartii*)	0.75m	0.5m	FS/PS
Babington's leek (*Allium ampeloprasum babingtonii*)	1.5m	0.2m	FS
Bellflower (*Campanula glomerata*)	0.1-0.5m	0.5-1m	FS/PS
Bergamot (*Monarda didyma*)	0.9m	0.5m	FS/PS
Betony (*Betonica officinalis*)	0.5-1m	0.1-0.5m	FS/PS
Bistort 'Superba' (*Bistorta officinalis*)	0.9m	0.5m	FS/PS
Borage (*Borago officinalis*)	0.6	0.3m	FS/PS
Broadleaf plantain (*Plantago major*)	0.1m	0.1m	FS/PS
Buck's horn plantain (*Plantago coronopus*)	0.3m	0.3m	FS
Burdock (*Arctium lappa*)	2m	1m	FS/PS
Carnation (*Dianthus caryophyllus*)	0.5m	0.5m	FS
Catmint 'Walker's Low' (*Nepeta racemosa*)	0.6m	0.5-0.75m	FS/PS
Chicory (*Cichorium intybus*)	1.5m	0.5m	FS
Chinese rhubarb (*Rheum palmatum*)	3m	2m	FS/PS
Chives (*Allium schoenoprasum*)	0.3m	0.3m	FS/PS
Cornflower (*Centaurea cyanus*)	0.75-1m	0.3m	FS
Courgette 'Gold Rush' (*Cucurbita pepo*)	0.5m-1m	1-1.5m	FS
Crocus 'Pickwick'	0.1m	0.1m	FS
Crocus, saffron (*Crocus sativus*)	0.1m	0.1m	FS
Daisy (*Bellis perennis*)	0.1m	0.1m	FS/PS
Dandelion (*Taraxacum officinale*)	0.5m	0.3m	FS/PS
Daylily 'Stella de Oro' (*Hemerocallis* sp.)	0.3m	0.3m	FS/PS
Daylily (*Hemerocallis fulva*)	0.5m	0.5m	FS/PS
Dwarf daffodil 'Hawera' (*Narcissus* sp.)	0.2-0.3m	0.1m	FS/PS

Plant name	Height	Spread	Sun/Shade
Dwarf tulip 'Everlasting Mixed' (*Tulipa* sp.)	0.4m	0.15m	FS
Dyer's coreopsis (*Coreopsis tinctoria*)	0.8m	0.2m	FS
Dyer's chamomile (*Cota tinctoria*)	0.5-1m	0.5-1m	FS
Early-flowering borage (*Trachystemmon orientalis*)	0.6-1m	1-2m	FS/PS
Echinacea (*Echinacea purpurea, E. pallida, E. angustifolia*)	1-1.5m	0.5m	FS/PS
Eupatorium 'Red Dwarf' (*Eupatorium maculatum*)	1.25m	0.5m	FS
Evening primrose (*Oenothera biennis*)	1-1.5m	0.5m	FS
Fennel (*Foeniculum vulgare*)	1.8m	0.5m	FS/PS
Feverfew (*Tanacetum parthenium*)	0.6m	0.3m	FS/PS
French marigold (*Tagetes patula*)	0.3m	0.3m	FS
Garden mint, aka spearmint (*Mentha spicata*)	1m	1.5m+	FS
Garlic cress (*Peltaria alliacea*)	0.5m	0.3m+	FS
Garlic mustard (*Alliaria petiolata*)	1m	0.4m	FS/PS
Geranium 'Rozanne'	1m	0.4m	FS
Geum 'Pink Petticoats'	0.25m	0.25m	FS/PS
Giant bellflower (*Campanula latifolia*)	1.5m	0.5m	PS/DS
Giant sea holly 'Silver Ghost' (*Eryngium giganteum*)	1m	0.5m	FS/PS
Globe artichoke (*Cynara cardunculu* Scolymus Group)	1.5m	1m	FS/PS
Globe thistle, blue (*Echinops bannaticus*)	1-1.5m	0.5-1m	FS
Globe thistle 'Veich's Blue' (*Echinops ritro*)	1m	0.5m	FS/PS
Goldenrod (*Solidago canadensis*)	1.2-1.8m	1m	FS/PS
Good King Henry (*Blitum bonus-henricus*)	0.5-1m	0.5m	PS/DS
Grape hyacinth (*Muscari armenicum)*	0.2-0.3m	0.1m	FS
Grecian bellflower (*Campanula versicolor*)	1.2m	0.5m	FS
Hemp agrimony (*Eupatorium cannabinum*)	1-1.5m	1-1.5m	FS/PS
Hooker's onion (*Allium hookeri*)	0.6m	0.1m	FS
Hosta 'Big Daddy' (*Hosta sieboldiana*)	1m	1m	PS/DS
Hosta 'Blue Angel' (*Hosta sieboldiana*)	0.9m	1.2m	PS/DS
Hosta undulata var. *Undulata*	0.4m	1m	PS/DS
Japanese anemone 'Robustissima' (*Anemone* x *hybrida*)	1.2m	0.5m	FS
Japanese indigo (*Persicaria tinctoria*)	1m	0.4m	FS/PS

Plant name	Height	Spread	Sun/Shade
Lady's mantle (*Alchemilla mollis, A. vulgaris*)	0.3-0.5m	0.6m	FS/PS/DS
Lamb's quarters (*Chenopodium album*)	0.9m	0.2m	FS
Landcress (*Barbarea verna*)	0.5m	0.3m	FS/PS/DS
Larkspur 'Limelight Light Pink' (*Delphinium consolida*)	0.9m	0.3m	FS
Lavender mint (*Mentha piperita f. citrata* 'Lavender')	1m	1.5m+	FS/PS
Lemon balm (*Melissa officinalis*)	1m	1m	FS/PS
Lemon verbena (*Aloysia citrodora*)	1-2m	1-2m	FS
Lupin 'Gallery Yellow' (*Lupinus*)	0.5m	0.5m	FS/PS
Madder (*Rubia tinctorum*)	1.5m	1.5m	FS
Marshmallow, (*Althea officinalis*)	1.2-1.5m	1m	FS
Masterwort 'Ruby Wedding' (*Astrantia major*)	0.5-1m	0.5-1m	FS/PS/DS
Masterwort 'White Giant' (*Astrantia major*)	0.5-1m	0.5-1m	FS/PS/DS
Meadowsweet (*Filipendula ulmaria*)	1.2m	0.4m	FS/PS
Montbretia 'Lucifer' (*Crocosmia* sp.)	1.6m	0.75m	FS/PS
Montbretia 'Red King' (*Crocosmia* x *crocosmiiflora*)	0.7m	0.5m	FS/PS
Mugwort (*Artemisia vulgaris*)	1.2m	0.7m	FS/PS
Mullein (*Verbascum thapsus*)	1.2-1.8m	0.4m	FS/PS
Nasturtium (*Tropaeolum officinale*), 'Empress of India' (*T. majus*)	0.3-0.5m	0.3-1m	FS
Nettle (*Urtica dioica*)	1-1.2m	1m	FS/PS/DS
Orpine (*Hylotelephium telephium*)	0.5m	0.3m	FS/PS/DS
Oxeye daisy (*Leucanthemum vulgare*)	0.6m	0.3m	FS
Peppermint (*Mentha* x *piperita*)	0.5m	1m	FS/PS
Perennial sunflower 'Lemon Queen' (*Helianthus* sp.)	2m	1m	FS
Perennial wall rocket (*Diplotaxis tenuifolia*)	0.6m	0.4m	FS/PS
Phlox 'Windsor' (*Phlox paniculata*)	0.9m	0.5m	FS
Pot marigold (*Calendula officinalis*)	0.6m	0.5m	FS/PS
Primrose (*Primula vulgaris*)	0.3m	0.3m	FS/PS
Primrose (*Primula pulverulenta*)	0.75m	0.5m	PS
Primrose (*Primula rosea*)	0.2m	0.1m	FS/PS
Primrose (*Primula veris*)	0.3m	0.2m	FS/PS

Plant name	Height	Spread	Sun/Shade
Red bistort 'Rosea' (*Bistorta amplexicaulis*)	1.2m	1m	FS/PS/DS
Ribwort plantain (*Plantago lanceolata*)	0.5m	0.2m	FS/PS
Rhubarb (*Rheum rhabarbarum*)	1m	1m	FS/PS
Rhubarb 'Glaskins Perpetual', 'Goliath', 'Stockbridge Arrow' (*Rheum* x *hybridum*)	1m	1m	FS/PS
Rudbeckia 'Goldsturm' (*Rudbeckia fulgida* var. *sullivantii*)	1m	0.5m	FS/PS
Rusty foxglove (*Digitalis ferruginea*)	1.5m	0.3m	FS/PS/DS
Sainfoin (*Onobrychis viciifolia*)	0.1-0.5m	0.1-0.5m	FS
Salad burnet (*Sanguisorba minor*)	0.6m	0.3m	FS
Salsify (*Tragopogon porrifolius*)	0.6m	0.4m	FS
Sea holly 'Jos Eijking' (*Eryngium* x *olivierianum*)	1m	0.5	FS
Scorzonera (*Pseudopodospermum hispanicum*)	1m	0.4m	FS/PS
Sedum 'Purple Emperor' (*Hylotelephium telephium*)	0.5m	0.5m	FS
Siberian bugloss 'Hadspen Cream' (*Brunnera macrophylla*)	0.75m	1m	FS/PS
Siberian bugloss 'Jack Frost' (*Brunnera macrophylla*)	0.5m	0.75m	FS/PS
Siberian iris (*Iris sibirica*)	1.2m	0.5m	FS/PS
Sneezeweed 'Moerheim Beauty' (*Helenium* sp.)	1m	0.5m	FS
Snake's head fritillary (*Fritillaria meleagris*)	0.5m	0.1m	FS/PS
Snowdrop (*Galanthus* sp.)	0.15m	0.1m	PS
Solomon seal (*Polygonatum multiflorum*)	1m	0.5m	FS/PS/DS
Sorrel (*Rumex acetosa*)	1m	0.1m	FS/PS
Star flowered lily of the valley (*Maianthemum stellatum*)	0.6m	1m	PS
Strawberry 'Buddy' (*Fragaria* x *ananassa*)	0.3m	0.3m	FS
Strawflower 'Granvia Pink' (*Xerochrysum bracteatum*)	0.5-1m	0.5m	FS/PS
Tree spinach (*Chenopodium giganteum*)	1.5-2m	1m	FS/PS
Turkish rocket (*Bunius orientalis*)	1m	0.75m	FS/PS
Udo (*Aralia cordata*)	2-2.5m	2-2.5m	FS/PS/DS
Valerian (*Valeriana officinalis*)	1.2m	0.75m	FS/PS
Verbena bonariensis	1.5-2.5m	0.5m	FS/PS
Weld (*Reseda luteola*)	1.5m	0.5-1m	FS/PS
Winter aconite (*Eranthis hyemalis*)	0.1m	0.1m	FS/PS

Plant name	Height	Spread	Sun/Shade
Woad (*Isatis tinctoria*)	1.2m	1m	FS
Yarrow (*Achillea millefolium*)	0.5-1m	0.1-0.5m	FS

Ground cover

Plant name	Height	Spread	Sun/Shade
Alpine strawberry 'Yellow Wonder' (*Fragaria vesca*)	0.3m	0.3m	FS/PS
Alpine strawberry (*Fragaria vesca*)	0.2m	0.2m	FS/PS
Big root cranesbill (*Geranium macrorrhizum*)	0.45m	1m	FS/PS/DS
Bugle 'Catlin's giant' (*Ajuga reptans*)	0.3m	0.5-1m	PS/DS
Bugle (*Ajuga reptans*), 'Variegata'	0.1-0.2m	0.5-1m	PS/DS
Chamomile (*Chamaemelum nobile*)	0.25m	0.4m	FS/DS
Clover (*Trifolium repens*)	0.1-0.5m	0.1-0.5m	FS
Comfrey (*Symphytum officinale*)	1.5m	1.5m	FS/PS
Dwarf comfrey (*Symphytum grandiflorum*) 'Hidcote Blue'	0.3-0.45m	1m+	FS/PS/DS
Garlic chives (*Allium tuberosum*)	0.3-0.4m	0.15m	FS
Golden marjoram 'Aureum' (*Origanum vulgare*)	0.3m	0.5m	FS/PS
Grape Hyacinth (*Muscari armeniacum*)	0.2m	0.1m	FS/PS
Iceland moss (*Sedum ternatum*)	0.15-0.2m	0.5m	FS
Korean aster (*Doellingeria scabra*)	1.2m	0.5m	FS/PS
Lemon thyme (*Thymus citriodorus*)	0.3m	0.3m	FS
Lungwort (*Pulmonaria officinalis*), 'Blue Ensign' (*Pulmonaria angustifolia*)	0.3m	0.5m	PS/DS
Oregano (*Origanum vulgare*)	0.5-1m	0.5-1m	FS/PS
Oregano 'Variegata' (*Origanum vulgare*)	0.5m	0.5m	FS/PS
Pachyphragma macrophylla	0.4m	0.5m	PS/DS
Pink purslane (*Claytonia sibirica*)	0.1-0.5m	0.1-0.5m	FS
Self-heal or heal-all (*Prunella vulgaris*)	0.3m	0.5m	FS/PS
Siberian bellflower (*Campanula poscharskyana*)	0.4m	0.5m+	FS/PS
Sweet violet (*Viola odorata*)	0.2m	0.3m+	FS/PS/DS
Thyme 'Silver Queen' (*Thymus* sp.)	0.3m	0.3-0.5m	FS
Violet 'Freckles' (*Viola sororia*)	0.25m		FS/PS
Wood Sorrel (*Oxalis acetosella*)	0.1m	0.3m	FS/PS/DS

Plant name	**Height**	**Spread**	**Sun/Shade**

Root crop

Plant name	Height	Spread	Sun/Shade
Camas (*Camassia quamash*)	0.3m	0.2m	FS/PS
Chinese artichoke (*Stachys affinis*)	0.5m	0.5m	FS/PS
Dog's tooth violet (*Erythronium dens-canis*) and *Erythronium* 'Pagoda'	0.25m	0.1-0.2m	PS
Garlic (*Allium sativum*)	0.6m	0.2m	FS
Jerusalem artichoke 'Fuseau' (*Helianthus tuberosus*)	2m	0.5m	FS/PS
Oca (*Oxalis tuberosa*)	0.5m	0.3m	FS
Wild hyacinth 'Caerulea' (*Camassia leichlinii*)	1-1.5m	0.5m	FS/PS
Yacon 'Inca Red' (*Smallanthus sonchifolius*)	1.8m	1m	FS

Climbers

Plant name	Height	Spread	Sun/Shade
Caucasian spinach (*Hablitzia tamnoides*)	3.5m	1m+	FS/PS
Chocolate vine (*Akebia quinata*)	8m+	2m+	FS/PS/DS
Cucumber, (*Cucumis sativus*)	2m	1m	FS
Dwarf hop 'Herald', 'Prima Donna', 'Sovereign' (*Humulus lupulus*)	3m	1.5m	FS/PS
Everlasting pea (*Lathyrus latifolius*)	2m	2m	FS/PS
Honeysuckle 'Sweet Sue' (*Lonicera periclymenum*)	3m	1m	FS/PS
Honeysuckle 'Winter Beauty' (*L.* x *purpusii*)	1.5-2.5m	1.5-2.5m	FS/PS
Honeysuckle (*L. periclymenum*)	4-8m	1.5m	FS/PS
Ivy (*Hedera helix*)	8-12m	1.5-4m	FS/PS/DS
Japanese Honeysuckle (*Lonicera japonica*)	8m	4m	FS/PS
Kiwi 'Jenny' (*Actinidia deliciosa*)	4-8m	2.5-4m	FS
Nasturtium (*Tropaeolum majus*)	0.5m	1m+	FS/PS
Peas (*Pisum sativum*)	2m	0.3m	FS/PS
Summer squash 'Trombonchino' (*Cucurbita moschata*)	2.5m	1m	FS

Index